THE

feng shui

DIRECTORY

THE
feng
shui
DIRECTORY

JANE BUTLER-BIGGS

with

ALISON DANIELS

WATSON-GUPTILL
PUBLICATIONS
New York

Library of Congress
Catalog Card Number: 00-105604

ISBN 0-8230-1657-9

This book was conceived, designed, and produced by
THE IVY PRESS LIMITED
The Old Candlemakers, West Street,
Lewes, East Sussex BN7 2NZ

Art Director: Clare Barber
Editorial Director: Sophie Collins
Designer: Jane Lanaway
Editor: Andrew Kirk
DTP Designer: Chris Lanaway
Studio Photography: Zul Mukhida, Guy Ryecart
Illustrations: Rhian Nest James
Mac Illustrations: Chris Mansbridge, Richard Constable
3-D Models: Mark Jamieson
Picture Research: Liz Eddison, Trudi Valter
Prop Researcher: Sarah Allaway

Printed by Winner Printing & Packaging Ltd in China

2 3 4 5 6 7 8 9 / 08 07 06 05 04 03 02 01 00
This book is typeset in News Gothic

contents

introduction

This book explains, in simple, common-sense terms, the basic philosophy that underlies Feng Shui and how it may be able to help in six key areas of everyday life: wealth and prosperity, love and romance, family harmony, health, career and the workplace, and happiness and well-being.

At the start of every section you will find questions to help you find out where you are in your life at this moment and assist you in defining your goals—not the ones imposed on you by the expectations of others, but the ones that will make you truly happy.

Each section ends with a few "Quick Fixes." There are no easy solutions in Feng Shui—it is a long-term, continuous practice—but treat these as Feng Shui first aid, to be used as remedies while you treat the underlying cause of the problem.

Above all, don't look to this directory for a set of rules that will mystically transform your life. It will point you in the right direction, but the onus is on you to do the work and change your inner and outer environments!

basics

Feng Shui has existed for more than 4,000 years. Can such an ancient philosophy still be relevant today? The answer is yes, because the Ancient Chinese who first developed it recognized that the universe is in a constant state of change and so Feng Shui would have to evolve to keep pace with it. But before you start to practice Feng Shui, you first have to learn the basics.

getting started

People often come to Feng Shui thinking it will transform their lives. It's true that introducing Feng Shui practices into your day-to-day environment can make a difference to the way that you live, but Feng Shui is not only an external, but also an internal, process.

QUESTIONS TO ASK YOURSELF

1. What is it you are hoping to get from reading this book?

2. Do you know what you really want out of life?

3. Are you looking for a set of rules to tell you how to transform your life?

4. Are you hoping to develop a new side of yourself that can become more conscious of the world around you and its effect on you?

5. Are you prepared to change with your environment?

FIRST, RELAX! In my work as a Feng Shui consultant, I often encounter people who are looking for a set of rigid rules by which to live their life. They've been misled by the media and the bewildering array of reference books, and think that if they position their bed at the right angle or place symbolic objects in the correct directional angle in their living room, their lives will suddenly and mysteriously change for the better. But Feng Shui doesn't work like that—it is not a fixed set of rules.

Don't be put off by an excess of information. Learn a few basic principles and follow your instincts.

NEXT, DEVELOP YOUR SKILLS Feng Shui is not a subject you can learn as a once-and-for-all template in how to arrange your environment or organize your life. It is an ongoing process, which should be approached minute by minute, hour by hour, day by day. It has to be adapted to suit your personality, your lifestyle, and your aspirations. It is not a practice that works when someone else dictates to you what to do; it is at its most effective when you develop it by yourself for yourself.

As well as possessing infinite variety, Feng Shui is also constantly changing over time. It is not a static concept, stuck in the past. The world today is a very different place from Ancient China, where the theory was born, but Feng Shui has evolved to reflect that, and is growing and developing all the time. The original concepts, however, still have value, because they can help people to organize their thoughts and structure their world in such a way that they can understand it and make better use of it.

Changing your environment can lead to changes in the way you live your life.

The principles of Feng Shui are not hard and fast rules. Many principles are common sense.

Everything is pushed against the walls so there is no focal point

Sharp edges create tension

Too many soft furnishings can absorb chi.

why practice
feng shui today?

People become interested in Feng Shui for a variety of reasons. The most common motivation is that they have become stuck in a rut and are hoping to jump-start their way out of it. Feng Shui is a good way of taking a fresh look at our habits and ways of being.

UNDERSTAND YOURSELF Feng Shui, like analysis or counseling, can help us to understand what makes us tick and recognize repetitious patterns of behavior, and through this knowledge, we can learn how to change our circumstances to help us achieve our goals. It enables us to take responsibility for our lives and helps us to create our own destiny, to take an active role in our own fate and not be a passive victim subject to the whim of others.

Feng Shui can be a catalyst for change when life seems to be going nowhere.

TAKE CONTROL The concept of taking control of our lives is a scary one. We all possess a lot of built-in resistance to change, and it often seems easier and more comfortable to do what other people expect and follow rigid rules imposed on us by parents, teachers, or even ourselves, than to rebel against them. We can then blame others when things go wrong. It's much easier to protest, "It's not my fault!" than to accept responsibility for your own actions and decisions.

LIVE YOUR LIFE It may seem selfish to decide to live life your own way. But increasingly today, people are becoming more aware of the way that their actions affect other people. Companies are becoming more conscious of the way in which stress and unhealthy office environments can affect staff welfare, and, in society, people everywhere are having to shoulder increased responsibility, working outside the home and maintaining and nurturing relationships within it. Added to this, the concept of karma and "what goes around comes around" is something a lot of us are now more conscious of.

By surrounding yourself with good energy, you can have a positive effect on the environment of those around you as well, enhancing the consequences of your own personal practice of Feng Shui. Most important of all, perhaps, is that although it may be a more challenging way to live, taking control of your own destiny is ultimately far more fulfilling than the alternative.

Invite prosperity and abundance into the present moment with positive energy.

Dreams can be fulfilled when you take action to move your life forward.

how can we use feng shui today?

There is a huge potential for change in the air with the advent of the new millennium, and there are wonderful opportunities to change a passive acceptance of the way things are into a better quality of life, in both the inside and outside worlds.

As we enter the Age of Aquarius, many people are taking a more spiritual approach to life.

COMMON BENEFITS Many people have been giving a lot of thought to the way they want to live their lives in the new century and, as a consequence, are seeking to bring about adjustments in their lives, whether it is in their relationships, career, or home. Feng Shui is not some kind of mystical set of rules which have no basis in reality. It is not based on arcane rituals; it is basic, everyday stuff that anybody can learn to use to their benefit. It requires no esoteric expensive purchases and is not the preserve of a privileged few; it is accessible to everyone and can help to support both individuals and society as a whole.

NEW BEGINNINGS In the same way that more and more of us are interested in keeping our bodies and emotions healthy, we can learn to look at how our environment affects us and take control of that as well. We must first understand what it's doing to us before we start to change things, and we should also take time to assess what is actually going on in our lives right now, so that we can accurately pinpoint the areas that need to be remedied and recognize the changes when they come.

A good time to instigate the practice of Feng Shui is either when you are thinking of moving or have just relocated, since a new environment will offer you an excellent opportunity to start to make radical changes in your life. If you are not looking for such drastic effects, however, it will be equally effective when gently introduced into your everyday routine.

MINDFUL PRACTICE When you first start to practice Feng Shui, take things very slowly. Don't introduce several changes simultaneously, because you won't be able to track their effects. Make one alteration to your environment and then wait to see how it feeds back into the rest of your life before you introduce any more. Come to grips with the fact that Feng Shui is an interactive process, rather than seeing it as a final statement given to you by somebody else imposing their ideas about how you should be living your life.

Also bear in mind that you cannot make mistakes. Contrary to what you may have read elsewhere, there is no such thing as good Feng Shui or bad Feng Shui. Different environments suit different people, and what works for someone else may not be effective for you. The important thing is to find out what does work for you.

Wind chimes help to slow down the flow of chi, or life energy.

Plants soften sharp edges, helping chi to flow unimpeded.

where it all started

The Feng Shui approach of using the design of living space to alter your life originates from Ancient China. The theory of Feng Shui—which means "wind and water"—came about from the Ancients' direct observation of the natural order of nature.

The Chinese symbol for water. Ancient Chinese philosophers believed that natural phenomena and living beings share the same vibrational energy.

TRADITIONAL FENG SHUI The Ancient Chinese built up a body of information about seasonal changes, directional influences, and cycles of food production, and the way these affected people's lives. Feng Shui was originally classified information, used as a tool of social control by the ruling Imperial court. That is why it is important not to get too rigidly stuck in traditional forms, because they don't always apply in today's modern world.

THE CONCEPT OF POWER While it originated as a means to maintain the minority power base, Feng Shui today has a much wider application and more positive

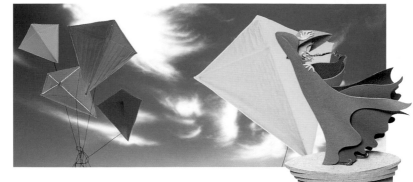

social implications. Nowadays, we are inclined to give power to individuals, rather than remove it from them, especially in the case of weaker members of society. Our view of power is different from that of the Ancient Chinese, and we recognize that it brings responsibility.

The symbol for wind, one of nature's most powerful forces.

MODERN ADAPTATION Some of the ancient Feng Shui rules on the building and design of houses are simply not workable today. We cannot guarantee everyone proximity to mountains and rivers, nor is it necessarily practicable— or desirable—to purchase a home only where the front door suits the chi of the head of the household!

Today's urban environments miss out on many advantages.

A NATURAL LEGACY The valuable Feng Shui legacy the Chinese have left us is the consciousness of our environment and the importance of constant observation, as well as philosophical concepts such as chi and yin and yang. We can continue the tradition of heightened consciousness, the respect for energy, and the basic theoretical models of Feng Shui. In respecting its origins, we should note that the Chinese were aware that change is the nature of life, and realize that Feng Shui must adjust to suit shifting circumstances.

the nature of chi

Different societies have different words for it—such as prana, ki, and chi—but all of them recognize that there is a life force that flows through us and through all the objects that surround us. As we move through the world, we are not self-contained beings.

THE ENERGY PRINCIPLE Most people would readily accept that there is a connection between us and other living things. However, we also have a connection with things that people in the West largely believe to be inanimate objects, such as mountains or streams. This concept is easier to grasp when movement can be directly observed, such as in clouds or a river. It's harder to believe when applied to tables and chairs! Yet scientists

Vibrational energy becomes obvious when you observe the gentle movement in natural scenery.

have proved that furniture, like everything else, is composed of atoms, which constantly vibrate. We can't see this with the human eye, but we know it to be true, so we might accept that they too possess an energy force.

CHI The Chinese called this elemental force *chi*. Although it is invisible, chi can be tracked; you can learn to recognize how it works. Chi doesn't move at a uniform pace; sometimes it can run too fast, sometimes it is sluggish or stagnant. To live your life at its optimum level, you need to be surrounded by the kind of healthy, free-flowing chi that is most conducive to the circumstances in which you find yourself at the time. Fortunately, it is possible to develop a sensitivity to chi and an awareness of how it moves, not only through people, but also through buildings, open spaces, and nature.

Sky and earth complement one another like the harmonious energies of yin and yang.

YIN AND YANG According to traditional Feng Shui, chi is divided into *yin* and *yang*—two opposing forces that are absolutely integral to each other, like two halves of a whole. If you look at the yin-yang symbol, you will see that each half contains a circle of its opposite, indicating that they are in a state of balance and harmony.

THE FIVE ELEMENTS The Ancient Chinese also broke chi down into the five elements. These are earth, fire, water, wood, and metal, and each has different distinguishing characteristics—but you will learn more about these later in this book.

yin and yang

The concept of the opposing energy forces of yin and yang is one that is absolutely central to an understanding of how Feng Shui works. With a little practice, you will soon learn to identify the yin and yang areas within your environment.

Yin (earth energy) and yang (heaven energy) are two balanced aspects of one whole.

COMPLEMENTARY FORCES What is the difference between yin and yang? Well, yin is diffuse earth energy, which rises up to the heavens, becoming more and more scattered, moving up and out as it ascends. It is cool and dark, and its nature is to facilitate flow, expansion, relaxation, and malleability. It can be seen as an embracing energy, which acts as a cup or basin in containing yang. Yang energy originates from the huge spaces of the heavens, and becomes more compacted and directed as it descends to earth. Hot and light, it is a very motivating force, which is also single-minded and inflexible, moving at speed.

OPPOSING ENERGIES When thinking about yin and yang, abandon the Western notion that one is somehow "better" than the other; they are just two different aspects of the whole. They are opposite forces with an element of each contained in the other, and everything is a balance between the two. It is only possible to have extreme yin if yang is also present, and vice versa. Without a context, you cannot have action and without action, you cannot have a context.

YIN AND YANG FOODS

The other important thing to bear in mind when contemplating yin and yang is that everything is relative. To take a simple example, think of yin and yang in terms of vegetables! A lettuce is a yin object, because it is diffuse, soft and malleable, while, when compared to lettuce, celery has a yang nature, because it is relatively compact and immovable. However, if you compare a stick of celery with a carrot, then the celery becomes yin while the carrot is yang, because the latter is a lot more compact and solid than the former.

A BALANCED ENVIRONMENT

The concepts of yin and yang are employed in Feng Shui for identifying the type of chi that would be most suitable to your environment. For example, you would not want the chi in a bedroom to be too yang, or you would not be able to enjoy restful sleep. Alternatively, if your study is too yin, you may find yourself daydreaming when you open your books, since this is obviously an area where a yang influence is desirable. Feng Shui can enhance the yin-yang nature of your environment to your optimum advantage.

Yin and yang are complementary, and vary according to their context.

Intellectual activities can be difficult in yin surroundings.

how we can work with chi

To practice Feng Shui successfully, you must first learn how to work with chi. That may sound like a daunting prospect, but there are a number of simple exercises you can do to develop your sense of chi.

Attitude and outlook can indicate the type of energy dominating someone's personality.

YANG PERSONALITIES First of all, try to identify forms of chi in other people. Think of five significant people in your life and work out what kind of chi each one possesses. Is she very active? Is she the kind of person who gets things done very quickly? Is she set in her ways and opposed to changes in her life? Is she very fiery and passionate? If the answer is yes, she may be a mostly yang person.

YIN PERSONALITIES Is he accepting of what life dishes out to him? Is he nurturing and supportive? Can he sometimes be a bit dreamy and irrational? Is he at his best in a creative environment or when giving help to others? These are the characteristics of a person who is mostly yin.

YANG CHARACTERISTICS You will find that when you know what to look for, there are ways of identifying whether complete strangers are yin or yang people. Yang people tend to have a compact body and their build is often short and stocky. When they enter a room for the first time, they look around in a very bold, direct way, select somewhere to sit immediately, move quickly toward it, and then seat themselves down confident that it is their rightful place in the room.

YIN CHARACTERISTICS Yin types tend to belong to a more elongated body and drape it in clothing that falls in soft lines. They will enter a room in a more diffident way, look around, and possibly even drift about the perimeter for a while before choosing a seat. Obviously, these are two very simplistic descriptions, but they do offer some basic guidelines—and remember that every person has a bit of yin and yang in them.

LEVELS OF CHI With a little practice, it is also possible to identify different types of chi within people. Those who have depressed or low levels of chi tend to be lethargic and can be difficult to motivate, while people with very sparky chi are full of ideas, and will appear bright and enthusiastic. If you always have several projects on the go and a tendency to lose things because there is a great deal of activity going on around you, you probably have dispersed chi, while a directed chi person is an expert at thinking ahead and planning for the future—and can often be a bit of a control freak!

YIN

YANG

The yang personality (left) is bold, confident, and direct. The yin personality (above) is softer and less assertive.

identifying the chi
in your environment

Once you have learned how to become sensitive to chi in other people, you can start to apply the same principles to the rooms that you live in. This is the first step in establishing how Feng Shui can improve your surroundings.

FINDING CHI PATHWAYS Look around the room you are currently occupying. Does it have any cluttered areas, where the flow of chi will get stuck? Are there bare and sparsely furnished areas, which chi will speed through? Are there gloomy corners where chi can stagnate?

Now decide on your favorite parts of the room. If there are areas which you particularly like, chi is probably flowing healthily there. Try to identify the features that you find attractive.

Hanging objects can gather dust, restrict energy flow, and encourage stagnation.

PRACTICAL TIPS Think of the different rooms in your home. What kind of room would you like to sleep in? Which one would you hold a party in? Which is most suitable for sitting in to do your accounts? Are these rooms suitable for the occupations you carry out in them? And if not, how could they be improved? Are they more yin or yang in their nature, and how does that affect you when you're occupying them?

When I start a consultation, I sit in the house for an hour, talking to its owner, and while I'm listening to him or her, I'm also alert to what the room is doing to me. This can be hard to do when you actually live in the house and are involved with it, so the following pages will give some guidelines to help you decide whether your space is yin or yang.

Spaces between furniture allow a free flow of chi to circulate around the room.

CASE STUDY

I once went into an office after another Feng Shui consultant had worked there and found it arranged in the most impractical fashion, with all the wastepaper baskets in the corners of the room, instead of under people's desks. Every time you wanted to throw something away, you had to leave your desk; the consultant had told them that all refuse should be put on the periphery of the room! To go to these lengths is really absurd. Remember, Feng Shui was never intended to make your life unnecessarily complicated or difficult!

yin and yang
rooms and houses

When identifying whether the rooms in your house are yin or yang, always remember that one is not "better" than the other. You will

want to keep all of the rooms in a state of balance, but at different times you will need to use one room more than another.

ROOM ENERGY Yin rooms are usually irregularly shaped and decorated in calm colors, with low furniture, scattered tables, subdued lighting, and possibly more than one door and/or windows. Yang rooms feature sharp angles, hard shiny surfaces, and white overhead lighting. They are usually decorated in plain colors or geometric or striped designs, and have a bright, sharp acoustic. There is usually only one entrance, and the room is task-oriented, its purpose very apparent.

This yang room has harsh lighting that casts sharp shadows. The shiny, angular surfaces are softened slightly by the plants.

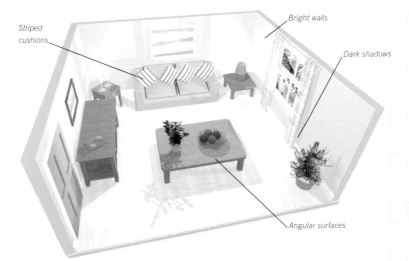

Striped cushions

Bright walls

Dark shadows

Angular surfaces

HOUSE ENERGY A yin house tends to be sprawling and low-level with hidden areas, with a hallway that runs crossways as you open the front door, curving walls, and arched windows. This is a good house for bringing up a family or growing old in, because of its relaxing nature.

A yang house would have a more regular, terraced design, with straight corridors running purposefully between the rooms and a standardized layout, with each room in the place that you would expect it to be. This would be a very good environment for a young, ambitious, career-oriented couple.

If you are living in a yang house with a young family, but seem to spend all your time working with little time to devote to them, you can introduce remedies to make it more yin. These include introducing curves, furnishing it with soft absorbent fabrics and reducing shiny surfaces and sharp edges. If you are living in a yin house and find that it is so relaxed that the occupants can never seem to get anything done, energize it with some yang elements such as polished wood floors or a high-tech kitchen, to wake everyone up!

This yin house is wide rather than tall, with curved bay windows and a curving corridor behind the central front door.

Shiny surfaces will magnify the energizing, yang qualities of a busy family kitchen.

different schools of feng shui

Various schools of Feng Shui coexist wherever it is practiced. This is a very healthy situation, because it keeps its practitioners constantly thinking about and reevaluating the contribution that any one school makes to the overall body of theory. The three main schools of Feng Shui are Form, Compass, and Intuitive.

Observation of the landscape encouraged in the Form School focuses the mind on becoming at one with our surroundings.

FORM SCHOOL This is the oldest, original school of Feng Shui, and its concepts rely heavily on looking at landscape, shape, texture, and structure. Its principles are very much based upon the act of long, slow observation, and are part of the Taoist tradition of not being intrusive and becoming at one with the object that is under observation. It has given us the whole concept of placement within a supportive environment.

COMPASS SCHOOL This school reminds us to work with universal energies and with heaven energy and to continue to track the way that chi flows through things from a universal perspective. It stops us from getting too preoccupied with what can be seen and makes us realize that we are affected by invisible influences as well as the observable. In other words, it keeps us alert to the metaphysical. A huge body of knowledge has been developed by the Compass School, and most Feng Shui books are based on this school, because it is relatively easy to define and tabulate.

INTUITIVE SCHOOL The third school acknowledges both of the other schools and brings them together. It uses the Form School concept of direct observation, but it also embraces the metaphysical aspects of the Compass School. Intuitive School is ready to take Feng Shui into the millennium. In a world where there is greater acceptance that the physical and vibrational worlds are linked, Intuitive School enables everyone to have access to Feng Shui, providing them with a tool to increase their understanding of their lives.

The metaphysical approach of the Compass School draws its inspiration from invisible universal energy.

The modern approach of the Intuitive School combines observation and inspiration.

employing a consultant

Hopefully, this book will give you guidance in practicing Feng Shui yourself. However, there may be occasions when you feel you need to engage a professional Feng Shui consultant, and there are a few things to look out for before making your choice.

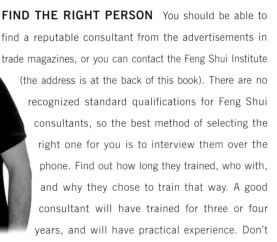

FIND THE RIGHT PERSON You should be able to find a reputable consultant from the advertisements in trade magazines, or you can contact the Feng Shui Institute (the address is at the back of this book). There are no recognized standard qualifications for Feng Shui consultants, so the best method of selecting the right one for you is to interview them over the phone. Find out how long they trained, who with, and why they chose to train that way. A good consultant will have trained for three or four years, and will have practical experience. Don't rule someone out who is self-taught, but do enquire about credentials and experience.

Finding a consultant is as easy as picking up the phone. Making sure the consultant is right for you takes a little more effort.

WHAT TO EXPECT Ask the consultant what she expects to do during the consultation, how long she will spend at your home, how much preparation she will do in advance, and whether she will research the astrology of the house's occupants. She should be prepared to spend time getting to know you and finding out what you want out of life. You should also find out what follow-up she will provide, because if you get results you don't expect, you need to be able to get some support.

BE INVOLVED Make sure there will be plenty of time to ask questions, and that the consultant will explain things to you fully rather than shrouding the whole process in mystery. If he can't explain it in a way you can understand, he probably doesn't understand it himself and is just working by rote! The consultation should feel like a very personal, considered evaluation of yourself and your whole life, not confined to bricks and mortar and the way to arrange your furniture.

Consider what it is you hope to get from the consultation; otherwise you might end up feeling dissatisfied without knowing why and having failed to communicate what you actually wanted from the session. And always be prepared at any point to decide that you will not take the consultant's advice if it doesn't feel right for you, as it is a very personal thing.

When living space is shared, a good consultant will spend time getting to know all the occupants of the house.

Feng Shui is not confined to choosing soft furnishings—it solves emotional issues by changing your environment.

good feng shui practice

When you decide to practice Feng Shui by yourself, you will need to follow some basic ground rules. Don't be afraid to experiment. You may be worried about doing something wrong, but whatever school of Feng Shui you decide to follow, if the intention is honest and honorable, the result will be good.

HAVE GOOD INTENTIONS Question yourself about your motives for practicing Feng Shui and have them clearly fixed in your head before you start. You cannot create a bad result if you are practicing with good intentions. Forget all of your fixed, achievement-oriented ideas, and do not operate from the concept that you will have to work hard or make some sort of sacrifice in order to achieve a worthwhile result. Good Feng Shui has to do with living in the present, so abandon any ingrained ideas you may have of delayed gratification and resolve to make the most of the here and now.

Trust your instincts. Problems in your surroundings can often be solved by listening to your intuition.

FOLLOW YOUR INSTINCTS Approach its initiation from the position that you are already a perfect Feng Shui person and that all you are actually doing is embarking on a process of remembering how to practice Feng Shui and getting back in touch with your instinct as to what works for you and what doesn't. Trust to that instinct in your heart and your head and don't be diverted from it, in spite of what other people tell you or of conflicting advice that you may read. You are the only person who knows what is right for you.

FORGET WISHFUL THINKING Think the whole process through very carefully, and don't expect that Feng Shui will assist you in achieving a specific goal, such as winning the lottery or meeting the partner of your dreams. It's not a cure-all magic wand, so don't use it in a goal-oriented fashion. Besides which, despite what you might tell yourself, possessing a fortune or getting married may not be the answer to all your problems. Remember the old adage: "Be careful what you wish for you might get it"!

The fulfillment of your dreams depends on the action you are prepared to take.

SEIZE THE MOMENT To get the most out of Feng Shui, you must learn to live in the present and nurture yourself now, instead of speculating on what tomorrow may or may not bring. So don't sit there worrying about how to arrange the room so that your love life blossoms in the future. Find a place in your room that makes you feel good right now. It's the slow building up of good quality chi in your life, both in your environment and inside yourself, that will attract blessings to you. So be prepared to live life to the max.

Building up good quality chi is as much a matter of nurturing yourself as it is about arranging the rooms in your house.

31

managing change

As you start to practice Feng Shui, it is important to honor the whole process, by closely observing the changes that you bring about. Employing Feng Shui successfully will always be an ongoing project and one which you can only learn about step by step.

UNDERSTAND YOUR RESULTS If you remove something from your environment that you are absolutely certain you need to get rid of, it can be incredibly valuable to work out exactly what effect that object was having on you, and in turn, it will give you the courage to make further changes when you understand the results you are achieving.

Making changes inevitably involves clearing out clutter, especially objects that hold you back by tying you to any troubles in your past.

GOOD EFFECTS Observe the time-lag between the actions you initiate and the results that develop, and make a note as to whether what you expected to happen actually did. Even if the effect was not what you anticipated, was the outcome perhaps better than you had hoped for? Maybe you were aiming to change your job, but instead won an unexpected promotion with your present employer, which may ultimately be more beneficial for you than moving to a new environment.

BAD EFFECTS You may find that the effect is something that you didn't want to happen. Perhaps you wanted to move chi around a room in your home more actively and so placed a large mirror on the wall—only to find that family arguments started to break out soon after. This means that the cure you employed was too strong and will have to be moderated to get the desired effect.

TAKE IT SLOWLY When you first start to practice Feng Shui, it is natural to be enthusiastic about it, but don't get carried away by immediately reaching for all the most powerful remedies at once. Treat yourself, the people around you, and the environment with respect. Curb your impatience and listen to your instinct when it comes to moderating the speed and range of remedies with which you work. If you use a whole series of cures simultaneously and you do get a result, you won't know which one has been the most effective, so you won't have learned anything from the experience that you can use again in your future practice.

Introducing too many changes at once can cause tension and confuse your thinking.

ACT WITH HONOR When you do start to achieve results, don't offer advice or point out errors in other people's environments. Feng Shui is supposed to empower the individual, and by telling other people what to do, you are taking their individual responsibility for their lives away from them.

KEEP UP THE GOOD WORK! First and foremost, remember that the best way to discover the secrets of successful Feng Shui is to practice it for yourself.

QUICK FIXES

1. Follow your instincts; you know better than anybody else what you need in your life.

2. Never practice Feng Shui for a negative reason; for example, because you're frightened or concerned. Always make changes for a positive reason.

3. Be kind to yourself; don't use Feng Shui as another stick to beat yourself with. Respect how well you've done up to now and continue to do so.

4. Be patient and don't expect Feng Shui to make instant changes in your life.

5. Don't let Feng Shui rule your life. As one of my teachers once said to me, "Don't put your life into Feng Shui; put Feng Shui into your life."

wealth and prosperity

They say money can't buy happiness... But in Feng Shui terms, the meaning of wealth and prosperity has far wider implications than the mere monetary. By using Feng Shui principles, you can help to bring abundance into your life and provide yourself with the kind of enrichment that will bring you true happiness.

all that glitters...

If you suddenly came into a lot of money, what would you be doing right now? Would you perhaps be sunning yourself on a beach in a tropical clime with a loved one for company? The Feng Shui view of wealth includes not only financial prosperity but also embraces an abundance of good things coming your way.

QUESTIONS TO ASK YOURSELF

1. How wealthy do you feel right now?

2. What do you consider to be wealth and prosperity?

3. If you were wealthy, imagine the environment you'd be in and picture how you'd feel.

4. What would make you feel prosperous? Is it money or something else, such as a loving partner?

5. Would you say that you are usually a fortunate or "lucky" person?

LIFE PRIORITIES Going back to the tropical beach scenario, think about which particular aspects of the scenario would make you feel fortunate. Would it be warmth? Freedom? Space? The company of someone you love? These are all things that most of us can enjoy here and now, without possessing a great deal of money, if only we take positive actions to create them.

Understand the motivation behind your dreams to bring them to fruition.

ABUNDANCE How abundant you feel has a lot to do with your point of view. Remember the old adage that a pessimist sees the cup as half empty, the optimist as half full. If you are living in a materially deprived situation but are surrounded by friends and are enjoying good health, you may feel either very poor or very fortunate, depending on your point of view.

What do you see first? The water or the emptiness above it?

POSITIVITY Equally, tough though it may be at the time, it is possible to interpret problems as gifts. While being laid off would normally be considered a very unlucky event, for some, the way in which family and friends rally around may make the person who has lost a job realize how loved and supported he or she is. And we all know of success stories about people who have used the opportunity to start their own business, resulting in greater wealth and personal satisfaction.

Abundance is about creativity and fulfillment more than material goods.

PROSPERITY Perception of prosperity also has a lot to do with the amount of control an individual has over her situation. If someone doesn't possess much material wealth but feels she could make changes to remedy that, she doesn't necessarily feel poor. For example, students revel in a lifestyle that has little material wealth but brings a lot of enjoyment and satisfaction. Feng Shui can help you to take control of your wealth and bring you prosperity in monetary and other, possibly more rewarding, ways.

making luck welcome

In order to attract prosperity, you have to set up your environment in a way that attracts good chi and allows it to enter your home. So the first thing you should do is to look at the approach to your home, because that indicates what you are inviting to come your way.

BE IMAGE-CONSCIOUS It can sometimes be very hard to look at your own home with objective eyes. What are you signaling to the universe? Are you presenting an abundant image to the world? Put yourself in the place of a visitor. When you are returning one day, stop 50 yards from your home, take out a notebook, and make two lists. On one, write down everything about your house that signals to the world that you are well-blessed and on the other, everything that relays that you are unlucky. Use this to build up the lucky message and look at ways of eradicating unlucky signs.

Living plants are symbols of vibrancy and energy.

The appearance of your house reflects your attitude to life.

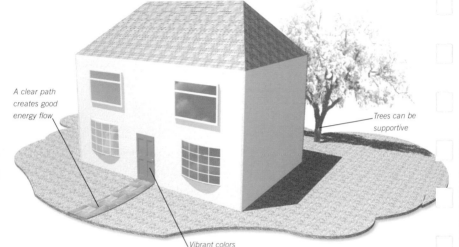

A clear path creates good energy flow

Trees can be supportive

Vibrant colors attract chi

INVITE GOOD CHI An attractive front garden, full of beautiful flowers, sends out the message that you rejoice in life, but you are not limited if you don't have space for one outside your door. Simply celebrate what you do have and build on what is at your disposal. Make your front door look attractive by painting it a bright color, keep your doorstep free of dirt, and polish the door knocker until it shines, to entice chi into your home. Keep the path to your front door free of clutter to encourage the flow of chi.

Living color celebrates life, and invites energy into your house.

OBSERVE THE RESULTS When you have done this, take a step back and observe what happens in your life and your home as a result. When you start to attract wealth and abundance, it's easy to become overwhelmed by it. You only have to look at the histories of various people who have won large sums of money to see how easy it is to become almost panic-stricken by unexpected wealth, because they don't know how to deal with it and may end up simply dissipating it with no long-term positive results.

Keep clutter and garbage away from paths where it cannot impede the free flow of chi into the house.

chi on the move

Once abundance has started to flow through your front door, you need to move it gently throughout your house, so your entire home absorbs all its nourishment and goodness. Think of it in terms of harboring healthy chi within your dwelling.

CREATE HARMONY   Chi should be able to flow without being broken up, scattered, or blocked, which means that the whole home needs to be harmonious in terms of decor, shapes, and design, with a smoothly running layout in order to assist wealth in coming to you.

CLEAR A PATH It's no good having a wide, welcoming front door if your hallway is dark and gloomy. Make sure that it is clear and bright and free of obstacles. All too often, halls become the dumping grounds for coats, boots, umbrellas, and bags. Make sure this area is kept tidy. The angles on coat stands break up the chi you've attracted

Keep coats and shoes neatly out of the way to create a path for the movement of chi through your hallway.

Pictures reflect life priorities and aspirations

Shiny objects reflect chi

Curved surfaces and plants encourage energy flow

Rectangular rugs direct the flow of chi

through the front door so you can't use it in a positive way, while items stored in the hallway—particularly large, shiny, metal objects—will bounce good fortune straight back out of the house again.

UPKEEP Clutter must be cleared regularly, since the entrances and exits of most homes tend to constantly attract it. Check your hallways at frequent intervals to make sure nothing has been dumped there.

CONSTANT CARE Remember that good quality chi must be cultivated all the time. It is not enough to simply attract it into your house, in the same way that it's not enough to know how to get a job by performing well in interviews—you then need to have a variety of skills and qualities in order to keep that job. Avoid having a cold spare room, a junk room, or otherwise neglected areas. Every part of your home must be equally loved and nurtured.

The hallway is the channel along which chi enters the home.

Energy upkeep requires the same attention you give to earning money.

slowing down chi

Once you've attracted chi into your house, don't allow a situation to occur where it runs straight out again. If chi flows through your house too fast, it won't be of any use to you; it will simply shoot through without bringing any benefits to bear.

THE BACK GARDEN If you have a big open garden through which chi might escape from the back of the house, make sure that there are some supportive elements in it that will hold onto the good luck. These elements could include a beautiful tree or shrub, or perhaps a lovely ornamental statue. They will support the back of the house and retain the healthy chi.

Beautiful potted plants at the front of the house help slow down the flow of chi.

DOORWAYS AND EMPTY SPACES Have a look at the way in which your garden gate, front door, and interior doors line up. If they are positioned in a straight line, a "tunnel" effect is created and chi will speed through the house. Stagger some tubs of plants along the front path to impede the flow of chi and decelerate it. To slow it down inside the home, rearrange your furniture, so that it can't simply pass straight through the rooms without bestowing any blessings. Another easy measure is to hang up pictures of dense environments. For example, instead of a painting of an open landscape, put up a picture of a beautiful walled garden; instead of a beach scene, choose a representation of a verdant forest. These will also have the desired effect of slowing chi down.

WINDOWS Beware of rooms that have double and triple exposures! This may sound strange because they are often beautiful rooms, which allow a lot of light into the home—but they can also allow chi to flow out of your house too fast. A good way to slow it down here is to arrange window coverings in layers. Drape swathes of muslin over them, or introduce dress curtains and blinds, or curtains with a valance, to slow chi down.

If your house is very yang, the energy will naturally move through it very quickly. If you are a motivated, ambitious person, this kind of house will suit you, but you shouldn't allow it to become too yang or the chi won't nourish you. Introduce yin areas to slow chi down; don't forget that yang must always contain yin, and vice versa.

Energy quickly flows out of large windows. Nearby external elements such as pillars and fences will slow its exit.

usable wealth

You may think that as far as prosperity is concerned, there is no such thing as too much! But you'd be wrong. In Feng Shui terms, if you are swamped with an overflow of wealth that comes in too fast, you either won't be able to use it at all or it will make your life miserable while you are trying to come to terms with it.

EVALUATE YOUR OPPORTUNITIES You may be looking to improve your abundance by applying for a new job, for example, or by trying to win a promotion. However, if you are offered a high-powered position that is well beyond your current capabilities, it will not prove to be a positive move for you. It will only create anxiety, stress, and strain, which will drain your energy supply and start to eat into your personal life, as you become more and more devoted to trying to keep up with the demands

Make sure that work challenges are within your capabilities. Inappropriate life changes can drain your energy.

of the new job. There is an alternative. Instead of taking the new job on, you may be wise enough to recognize that this new opportunity is likely to occupy far too much of the precious time that you would like to spend with your young family and friends. This realization—that the high-powered lifestyle may not suit you at the moment—may give you the courage to turn the job down.

SLOW THE FLOW If the opportunities that are coming into your life do not really result in abundance, look around at your environment to see how much chi is flowing into it. Perhaps you have chosen or created a house where too much chi comes in through the front door, overwhelming you with too many opportunities and presenting you with challenges that are simply too ambitious for you to take on at present.

It is, of course, also possible that this situation may have arisen through the over-enthusiastic application of Feng Shui. Maybe you cut down the trees at the front of the property, hoping to open up your prospects, without thinking about the potential strength of the results. Chi may now be flooding into your home in such quantities that you find it impossible to cope with your new situation.

By standing outside your front door looking in you will see what messages you are sending to the universe.

Overenthusiasm can bring unforeseen consequences.

PRACTICE MODERATION The danger of moving beyond your ability to cope is one of the reasons why you should always practice Feng Shui in a careful, measured way. If you do want to open up your prospects, cut down one tree and then wait to see what happens before you start on another. I've said it before, but it bears repeating: you must always remember that Feng Shui remedies must be appropriate to your situation. You have to take great care to match your requirements to your environment.

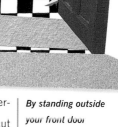

getting the balance right

I've already talked about the importance of chi being able to flow unimpeded and also of it having the right quality. However, in order for you to use chi in a way that enriches every aspect of your life, it has to be present in a balanced form.

FLOOR PLANNING Chi needs to support every part of you, not just certain aspects of you, otherwise this will be echoed in your environment. If you realize that, from the point of view of others, you may be considered wealthy or prosperous, but you don't feel as if you are, it may be that there's an imbalance in your life, and that would be reflected in the shape of your living space. To identify this, draw a floor plan of your living space. It doesn't have to be accurate and measured with a ruler, it can just be the way you perceive it to be. You can sketch it out in a few minutes, on the back of an envelope if you like!

The balance of your floor plan can give you clues about changing the layout of your internal space.

LOOK FOR IMBALANCE Square or rectangular houses are the easiest to remedy from the Feng Shui point of view, so look at the floor plan you have drawn, and see if it reflects balance, or irregularity and absence. Irregularity will show up as areas that jut out from the rest of the building, such as extensions, destroying the

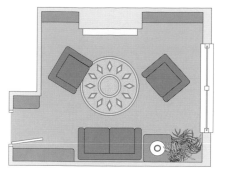

Floor Plan A: an extension causes irregularity in a room.

regularity of the square or rectangle. (See Floor Plan A.) Absent space takes the form of "missing corners," or areas bitten out of the regular square/rectangle shape. (See Floor Plan B.)

NOTICE FLOOR SHAPES If part of your living space protrudes outside the rest of your home's regular shape, it emphasizes certain parts of your life. If

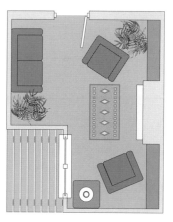

Floor Plan B: cutaway areas cause problems with absent space.

there is an area that is physically missing, it reflects the fact that part of your life, as well as your environment, is not being nurtured properly. Either way, it indicates that an imbalance is present and needs to be remedied.

You don't necessarily have to understand which facets of your life you're emphasizing or exaggerating, or where there is lack (although often it may be immediately obvious to you; for example, if the absence is in your study, you may find it hard to settle down to work). What you do need to do is to address the irregularity and restore the balance. Luckily, Feng Shui remedies can help you to achieve this by suggesting several useful ways of squaring off the floor plan.

remedying irregularities

If the floor plan of your living space has one or more missing corners, there are a number of ways in which you can compensate for this "absent space," make a room more regular, and help to balance the chi within your environment.

Uncluttered corner units can help to energize a room by softening its edges.

DECOR AND LIGHTING In remedying a room with absent space, you should aim to boost the energy level internally, and to prevent stagnation from occurring. You can do this by decorating it with bright colors and keeping window dressings to a minimum to allow light in. Also empower the room before the absent space to energize it with more yang. You can do this by clutter-clearing; taking away some of the soft furnishings; if you have shelves that are covered by a door or curtain, remove the covering so they are open in the room; reduce the amount of blinds at windows; turn downlighters into uplighters; add task lights; paint surfaces with a gloss rather than a matte finish. Meanwhile keep the room beyond the absent space very clear and calm, with a more subdued decoration, which will help to balance the irregularity.

MIRRORS Some Feng Shui consultants suggest using mirrors to correct absent space, but I always advise amateur Feng Shui practitioners to be careful, since these can be very powerful chi movers. However, if you do want to experiment with this remedy, try placing a new, framed mirror on the wall dividing the absent space from the room before it. If that is not possible, place a mirror on

Mirrors reflect chi, but their effects can be very powerful, so be careful where you place them.

the wall dividing the absent space from the room which follows it, facing the mirror into that room.

Once absent space has been remedied, people often find that their experience of their situation greatly improves, and they can then receive the full impact of an easy flow of abundance and good fortune. They may actually begin to feel much wealthier, even though their material position may not have altered at all.

PATIOS AND PLANTS Areas that jut out from the rest of the house are more difficult to remedy, but the best way to try to do it is by constructing a terrace or patio, or just placing a plant in a container or some garden furniture, in such a way that it squares off the floor plan. It is important not to make a room that contains irregular areas the most active room in the house. Try to keep it as a study or music room, or ideally a guest bedroom, so that you are actually pulling chi out of it.

Where parts of a house jut out, container plants can help to square off the floor plan on the outside.

banishing poverty

In attracting wealth and prosperity, you need to remove objects which symbolize poverty, or at least imply a lack of abundance. Keeping items such as a vase that has been broken and glued back together again, crockery that is chipped, or door handles that don't turn anymore all signal to the universe that you are prepared to accept less than the best.

Broken crockery should be thrown away or replaced.

Signal to the universe that you expect the best for yourself.

REPLACE OR REMOVE! Look around your immediate surroundings and reduce all symbols of poverty. These are often broken or worn-out things that you may have not got around to replacing. Even if you can't afford to replace things at the moment, do without them altogether rather than keeping them in your home.

MAKE YOUR MARK Suppose, for example, you still use the shabby curtains you inherited when you moved into your house. If they are not to your taste and don't reflect what you have to say about life, they should be replaced. If a pair of new curtains is currently outside your financial reach, take the old curtains down and do without them, leaving the windows bare rather than putting up with them for the time being. If you keep them up, they give out a strong signal that you are generally prepared to "make do" with whatever you're given rather than seek out abundance for yourself. Remember that everything in your immediate environment reflects your taste and your outlook on life.

OWN SOMETHING BEAUTIFUL Some of my Feng Shui consultations involve looking at the homes of people who are worried about their lack of money and material goods. When I visit these places, I regularly find that the occupants have surrounded themselves with powerful symbols of deprivation and impoverishment, and cannot break out of a negative cycle of thought. It is well worth spending limited resources on one really beautiful item, like a well-designed cup or vase, as a means of starting to introduce prosperity into your environment. You could invite abundance into your life by altering your negative outlook.

A single beautiful object can attract more abundance and beauty into your life.

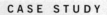

CASE STUDY

I was once called in to help a lady who was struggling financially and felt very impoverished in every area of her life. She lived in a basement appartment with the entrance around the side of the main building. Her front door pointed out to the perimeter of the plot, facing a fence. In her state of depression, she'd allowed the garden to become very overgrown, so I literally had to bend double to get to the door. No wonder healthy chi couldn't penetrate the tangled weeds and brambles! Looking around the inside of the flat, I noticed in the kitchen cluttered shelves that were full of half-empty, dusty jars—another obvious symbol of neglect. I advised her to tidy up the garden to allow easier access, and to remove the jars from the shelves, replacing them with prettier things. After she'd done this, things gradually improved to the point where she had enough money to buy the ground floor appartment, giving her access to more daylight and a much healthier environment.

do you deserve
to be wealthy?

When you read **Question 3 at the start of this section (page 36)**, what kind of situation did you envision? Taking yourself back there in your mind's eye, list five of the features that are currently within your reach. What is behind you? What is in front of you? What can you hear? What can you smell? What can you feel?

What positive images do you associate with rich scents?

Which elements of natural beauty do you wish to reflect in your home surroundings?

CHANGE YOUR SCENERY Perhaps you are reveling in the warmth of the sun on your back. Maybe you are sitting in a lovely garden, enjoying the beauty of the flowers and inhaling their scent. You might be listening to your favorite kind of music or simply having enough leisure time to sit and play with your dog.

OBSERVE YOUR THOUGHTS As you picture that wealthy environment, absorb the nature of it and then think about whether there are any of those five elements you identified in your current situation. Which of them do you feel you deserve to have in your life? If you feel that you are not worthy of one or more of them, ask yourself why not, and what's in the way that prevents you from thinking you deserve them?

Now undertake some practical Feng Shui to unlock the beliefs that you are not worthy of prosperity and/or that you can't attain it. Use it to make real changes in your everyday life that you can't make internally.

Believing that you deserve prosperity will open your life to it.

TAKE ACTION Do this by finding a way in which you can incorporate each of those five elements you imagined into your current environment. If part of your wealthy environment was the smell of flowers, go out and buy yourself some. If it was the warmth of the sun on your back, pay attention to making your current living space cozy and draft-proof. Don't restrict it to one room, but distribute this wealth throughout your home and your workplace.

Enjoying life is a skill that develops from positive thinking.

INVITE SUCCESS By carrying out this exercise, you are introducing the possibility that you can enjoy wealth. Additionally, it has the bonus that it is your own version of prosperity, the kind of wealth that suits you at this time in your life, not some externalized version.

tuning your outer space for wealth

Feng Shui is not just something that happens inside your head; it is all about practical action. The great thing about Feng Shui is that it is something you can practice every day on a real level to help you

move toward your dreams. Here is a practical form of action that you can carry out to locate the abundant environment both within and without and to help it to manifest itself in the present.

Clear out books and magazines that you no longer read.

FIND THE RIGHT DIRECTION First, choose a south-facing room within your home. If you don't have a south-facing room, choose an east-facing, or failing that southeast-facing room—but south is best for this ritual.

CLEAR OUT CLUTTER To tune your outer space for prosperity, you must completely clear out any clutter in your chosen room, so that chi can flow unimpeded.

Put aside any unfinished projects so as to concentrate on the present.

Remove from the room any items that have a connection to your past difficulties. You are concentrating on the present moment and on your aspirations for the future. Also clear away any objects that are broken, or projects that have been abandoned or are incomplete. Any ongoing projects that are not yet finished should be moved into another room.

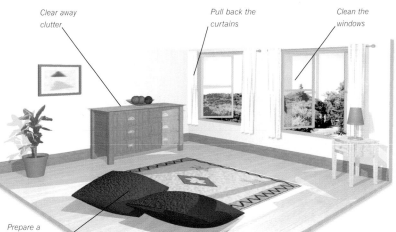

Clear away
clutter

Pull back the
curtains

Clean the
windows

Prepare a
comfortable
place to sit

PREPARE THE SPACE

Clean the windows inside and
out, open them, and pull the curtains back and the blinds
up, even if you intend to carry out the ritual at night.

The next part of the preparations is to energize some
water. You do this by leaving a bowl of water on the
windowsill for 24 hours, so it is there throughout a whole
cycle of the sun and moon. Put the water in a plant
sprayer, and, every day, before you commence the ritual,
walk around the room and spray the perimeter with it.

FIND A SEAT Choose the place where you are going to
sit and what you are going to sit on. Whether you decide
on a chair, a cushion, or a mat, during the period that
you are continuing to carry out the ritual, don't use it
for anything else.

Once you have completed all
these preparations, you are ready to
tune your inner self for wealth.

*Prepare the room
carefully before
beginning your ritual.*

*The seat you choose
should only be used
for energy rituals.*

tuning your inner space for wealth

If you want to have abundance manifest itself within your life, you have to be serious about it. This means that you must find time

within your life to focus on this exercise every day within a certain period of time.

To change your life, you must devote time to taking action.

Full moon is a time with great potential for change.

CHOOSE YOUR TIME Before you start to tune your inner space for wealth, you have to make a number of decisions. First, ascertain how long you can spend on the ritual every day; whether it is five or 20 minutes, the choice is yours. Then choose a time of day when you know you are always full of energy and positive feelings; that is the time that you should carry out your ritual. Finally, fix yourself a time limit. Twenty-eight days—one complete cycle of the moon—is a good one, and if possible, try to start the ritual with the new moon.

RECORD YOUR INTENTION Take a clean piece of paper and date it. Then try to work out a very clear intention about what it is you are trying to do. If you are uncertain how to define your wishes, read over the questions at the beginning of this chapter again to help you to clarify your thoughts. Once you have resolved what your intention is, reduce it down to one sentence with three key words. Here are some examples to help you:

"I want to be **abundant** and **prosperous** now." Or: "I want to feel that I have adequate **resources** to **fulfill** my **dreams**."

When you have written down your sentence, highlight the three power words, as I have in these examples.

Use a pen and paper to record your intentions in black and white. This will help your resolve.

FOCUS YOUR MIND You are now ready to start. All you have to do is spend your five or 20 minutes every day, at the appointed time, throughout the length of your chosen period, sitting in your chosen place and focusing on those words.

It can also be a good idea to introduce into the room an object that symbolizes one or more of the power words. So if your dreams involve travel, you could bring in a picture of a place you'd like to visit. If your dreams involve having enough money to enable you to follow your passion for art, placing some fresh paints in the room may be beneficial.

You will find that this exercise helps you to really focus on prosperity and start to make it real for you.

Symbols of your power words can focus your mind.

QUICK FIXES

1. Check that the end of the yard isn't a mass of broken flowerpots and brambles.

2. Sweep your doorstep and wash it with water with rose or jasmine oil in it if possible.

3. Sweep the front path with a new broom, if you can afford to buy one.

4. Polish and clean windows all around the house.

5. Replace all of your light bulbs, so no broken ones are left in place.

LOVE AND
ROMANCE

love and romance

Whether you've always been "unlucky in love," are having problems attracting a mate, or are in a long-term relationship that seems to have run out of steam, Feng Shui can help you to enrich your love life. By making physical changes to your living space, you also make emotional changes. It's all a question of balance.

soulmate or friend?

The ancient philosophers who first propounded Feng Shui theory subscribed to the idea that marriage was the most desirable state to live in! Many people today also feel that it is vital to find the right life partner.

A successful partnership demands that you make time for one another. Is there room for another person in your life?

QUESTIONS TO ASK YOURSELF

1. Are you happy with the state of your love life?

2. Are you looking for a partner for life or would "serial monogamy" suit you better?

3. Have you got so many things going on in your life that you wouldn't have the time to see a lover more than once a week?

4. How far are you prepared to compromise your independence to accommodate a partner?

5. Are you in a long-term relationship that has gone stale and lost its excitement?

SOCIAL PRESSURES   Despite having a successful career and a wide circle of friends, many people feel a failure if they do not have a long-term partner beside them. In the modern world, through media, advertising, and social pressures, we are continually bombarded by the message that we can only become complete when we find a soulmate.

LIFELONG COMMITMENT? Whatever the social pressures, a lifelong partnership is not an arrangement that suits everybody. While for some it may be nirvana, it can seem like a life sentence to others! So before you start to use Feng Shui to remedy your love life, ask yourself what you really want to obtain from it. Do you want to share your living space with a partner on a permanent basis, or would you prefer to see a boyfriend or girlfriend on a more casual, dating basis—or maybe you are so involved and fulfilled in your career that you would just like to have someone to hang out with during weekends and on vacation? Once you've sorted out the kind of mate you want, you can then direct your use of Feng Shui remedies more effectively to help to attract the right type of person.

The Chinese symbol for Earth. Earth energy can make or break a relationship.

RELATIONSHIP PROBLEMS Difficulties in love and relationships are caused by an imbalance in chi—and primarily, that is usually an imbalance in the area of earth energy. Earth energy is the most fundamental of the five components of chi, as defined by the Chinese—and unfortunately, it is often the element that is more depleted in those of us who live in the West. Before we can start to remedy earth energy, however, we must first understand what this type of energy is, what its properties are, and how it relates to the other four elements that make up chi.

If you have time for others only on weekends, long-term commitment may not be right for you at present.

earth energy

As human beings, we stand between the heavens and the Earth. We can move freely between the two, but while we take our inspiration from the heavens, we are connected to the Earth down through the ground for our own stability.

Growing up in an atmosphere of love and security keeps us in touch with our earth energy.

A NOURISHING RESOURCE Earth energy deals with this connection, and is all about getting in touch with the universe's natural rhythms and cycles and the place that we occupy in the great scheme of things. It is also about the way in which living beings draw nourishment from the Earth. Earth energy is demonstrated on a day-to-day basis by our ability to use all the resources that are available to us. An important aspect of this is the good things about our upbringing, or the support that we "fed on" as a child.

NATURE AND NURTURE A simple way to understand how earth energy affects us is to picture ourselves as a plant. To grow in a healthy way, it needs to be planted at the right time in nourishing soil, and must develop at an appropriate rate. A plant that has been either overfed or starved during its period of growth will not be strong or vigorous when it reaches maturity. Similarly, the way we come into the world and are nurtured in our early life will manifest itself in our earth energy in adulthood.

DIFFICULT BEGINNINGS To be able to use our resources properly, we have to believe that we have the right to be here, and this conviction is nurtured when a child grows up secure in the knowledge that he or she is wanted and loved. When an individual's earth energy is out of kilter or deficient, it is often related to a lack of support in formative years. Although a plant that has not been properly nourished will still flower, it is spindly and blows around in the wind. Similarly, despite the fact that someone who experienced emotional deprivation in childhood may appear to be "blooming," he or she is actually depleted at the roots of being, and this lack of nourishment results in a constant struggle for support and love. Those suffering from this imbalance in chi may have relationship problems because they don't feel centered or possess little self-esteem. The best way to balance their chi is to go back to their roots and get in touch with their natural rhythms and cycles.

If we were not strongly rooted during childhood, this will cause emotional struggles in later life.

the cycle of elements

Ancient Chinese philosophers believed that chi is manifested in five basic elements—fire, earth, metal, water, and wood—and that these must all be present in a balanced way in an individual's life cycle. One or two, however, will predominate at different periods.

FIRE

WOOD

EARTH

PRODUCTIVE CYCLE

EACH ELEMENT CREATES THE NEXT IN THE CYCLE

WATER

METAL

Harness creative energy with the first cycle.

WATER

EARTH

FIRE

SHAPING CYCLE

EACH ELEMENT SHAPES THE NEXT IN THE CYCLE

WOOD

METAL

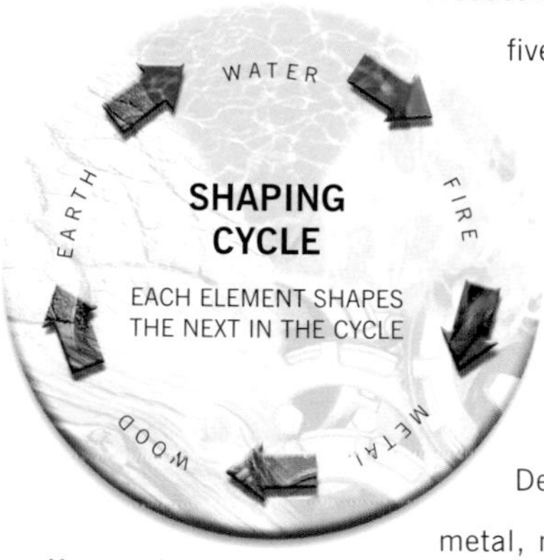

Harness shaping energy with the second cycle.

INTERACTION The elements are not fixed; they are fluid, transforming principles, which interact together to create an object, an event, or a situation. They boost and build each other, and they also shape each other.

THE PRODUCTIVE CYCLE The Chinese philosophers expressed the relationships between the elements through the two diagrams you see here. The diagram above illustrates a concept known as the Productive Cycle, which describes how each of the five elements affects the others; fire creates earth, earth is used to produce metal, metal holds water, water nourishes wood, and wood feeds fire.

THE SHAPING CYCLE The second cycle is often referred to as the Destructive Cycle: it shows how fire melts metal, metal cuts wood, wood consumes earth, earth soaks up water, and water douses fire. However, I prefer to think of it as the Shaping Cycle, because its principles do not have to be interpreted as negative processes. For example, metal in the form of an ax can be used to shape wood into a useful or decorative object. Similarly, if a person has an excess of wood energy, which relates to planning, she will always be looking ahead and will not be settled in the moment. The introduction into their life of more metal energy, which is associated with leisure, will calm them down.

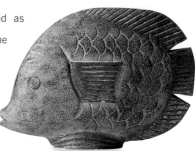

A beautiful object can arise from the "destructive" force that cuts down the tree.

Once you understand how the five elements interact within the Productive and Shaping Cycles, you can use them to moderate the earth energy within your life and correct any imbalances.

THE FIVE ELEMENTS

ELEMENT	COLOR RANGE	COMPASS DIRECTION	ACTIVITY
Water	Blue Navy blue Black	North	Contemplation Quiet Deep power Sexuality
Wood	Green	East	Growth Development New ideas Planning
Fire	Red Flame colors	South	Action Enlightenment Self-esteem Public status
Earth	Yellow Natural earth colors	Center	Relationships Nurturing Ability to be centered Resourcefulness
Metal	White Silver Gold	West	Order Structure Leisure and pleasure Creativity

balancing the five elements

Because all five elements work together, you cannot boost one area without looking at all the others, otherwise you will either be exacerbating the current imbalance in chi or creating another one. So in order to balance your earth energy, you need to look at all the other elements in relation to it, the key one being fire energy.

The Chinese symbol for Fire, which is linked to activity and excitement.

FIRE ENERGY   Excitement and good times are associated with fire energy, and are essential if you want to nurture and nourish yourself. If you are unable to deal with your earth energy issues, they may relate to unresolved issues from the past. You need to feed earth with fire when fire is depleted, so boost your fire energy by making sure you find time to have fun. And, just as wood, which is associated with planning, feeds fire, so you can increase your wood energy, as well as enhancing your enjoyment of life, by organizing an outing or a party.

METAL ENERGY   You can drain off any excess earth energy with metal energy. Metal energy is also associated with pleasure, but of the habitual type rather than the transient variety, as well as being concerned with being kind to yourself and letting go of things that are bothering you. It is to do with structure and from that, completion, so make sure the tasks you undertake are finished off. Once you've thought through the problems of your childhood, draw a mental line under them; look at the strength you gained from surviving difficulties and don't spend any more time dwelling on them. Or, if you're implementing some of the earth energy remedies you'll read about later in this section and you've taken them as far as you can, tell yourself that you're done with them for now and move on.

WATER ENERGY Also remember that earth energy has a role to play in shaping the water energy in your life. Water energy is about allowing yourself to be still and quiet. You may be sitting meditating, looking inactive to the casual observer, but really, inside your head, there's lots going on. Water energy is often compared to a garden in winter, which looks dead, while down in the ground, the bulbs are gradually working their way up to the surface. As you're about to find out, this time of apparent inactivity is an important part of the natural cycle of life, and leads to new growth later on.

The Chinese symbol for Metal, which is linked to long-term pleasure.

Physical inactivity allows time for your mental processes to get to work.

to everything, there is a season

Different elements are associated with different seasons; fire is related to summer, metal to autumn, water to winter, and wood to spring, while earth mediates the changes between them. Everything, including relationships, has a seasonal cycle, and we should honor every phase of it.

Ancient Chinese philosophy states that everything in the universe is made up of five basic elements.

FIRE 火

EARTH 土

WOOD 木

METAL 金

WATER 水

TRANSIENCE The early stages of a relationship are the fire or summer phase; fire is associated with passion, which burns bright when two people first fall in love with each other. Inevitably, it is followed by the metal or autumn phase, when the initial throes of love and lust start to subside into a quieter period. Many people are dismayed when this happens, because they think something is going wrong with the relationship, and, instead of allowing it to naturally move on to the water or winter phase, they try to turn the clock back and transform it into summer again. At this point, many relationships break up, because it appears to those involved that the excitement has disappeared from their affair.

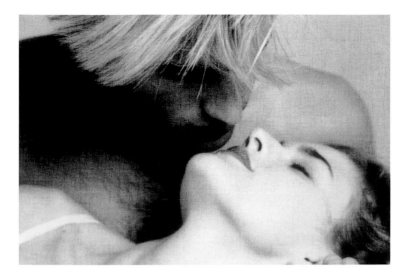

FULFILLMENT During the water/winter phase couples enjoy the quiet contentment of deep emotion, and can spend an evening happily engaged in separate activities in the same room, barely speaking but still enjoying each other's company. This will eventually turn into the wood/spring phase, when the relationship is ready to move on.

Weathering phases or "seasons" together is part of maintaining a loving relationship.

TRANSITION If your earth energy isn't in balance, your relationship can get stuck in one particular phase or season. If you can't move past the fire/summer phase, the level of passion eventually proves unsustainable, and if you get inextricably wedged in the water/winter phase, you can become bored by the lack of activity. If your earth energy is balanced, you will sense when you are about to move from one phase to the next; if it is depleted, you may not have the resources to make the transition, and that's when a relationship can die. Think of earth energy as the big gearing system of chi, and you'll appreciate what an important role it plays in your love life.

unlucky in love

When I visit a home where the inhabitants are having problems maintaining a relationship, I expect to see signs of imbalance everywhere. These basically reveal that there is a corresponding imbalance of chi. In other words, chi isn't supporting two people equally; it will only support one at the expense of the other.

EXTERNAL SIGNALS Viewed from the outside, a classic example would be that the exterior of the house has an extension added to one side, which unbalances it, or it might be built on a sideways slope, so one side is built up while the other falls away. One area of the garden may be very neatly cultivated, while another is left to grow wild, or one very big tree may be overshadowing a tiny bush. In some flowerbeds, plants may be thriving, while in others, shrubs struggle to survive.

Shabby or confused decor is a signal of an energy imbalance, which can make relationships very difficult to sustain.

INTERNAL SIGNALS Inside, one may find that while some rooms are beautifully decorated and completely finished, in others no work has been done at all since the occupants moved in, and they look drab and shabby in comparison. Styles of decor within the house may also contrast sharply; one room may be very feminine, with lots of frills and flounces, painted in pastel shades, while another is very masculine, full of straight lines and with a clinical feel.

Hallways, passageways, and landings may be left bare and show signs of breakages, such as cracked windows and mirrors, clocks that no longer work, and peeling plaster in the corners—all indicating that the links between the inhabitants have ruptured.

Cracked mirrors turn away abundance and signal a general lack of communication.

The balance of power in your relationships reveals itself in your surroundings.

THE BALANCE OF POWER All of the above reveal that obstacles are getting in the way of a balanced relationship. If you see these signs of imbalance around your home, you have to ask yourself how much you are prepared to put into maintaining the relationship. How much power are you ready to give away? Look at ways to distribute the energy held between you. Would you be happy to take a more passive role? You should think hard about the balance of power within a relationship that would be right for you before you attempt to correct your earth energy.

out of bounds

There are other, very obvious signs that indicate that chi is out of kilter. One of these is a noticeable lack of boundaries—between inside and outside, between peace and activity, between light and dark, between ourselves and others.

Boundaries are important for conserving earth energy, so take care to repair broken fences and gates.

FUZZY BOUNDARIES Our sense of self relies on knowing where our center is and our limits lie. If we are unsure about our sense of worth, this will be reflected in fuzzy boundary lines around our living space. So, with a house where earth energy is unbalanced, it may not be clear where the property begins and ends. Fences may be broken and gates will be hanging off their hinges.

When a Feng Shui consultant enters such a house, he or she might expect to see overflow between the functions of the different rooms, so, for example, a computer will be set up in the kitchen, which ought to be the home's focal point for food preparation, or a rowing machine will be stored in the bedroom, which should be devoted to relaxation and sleep. It is often likely that objects will be on the move between rooms; there may be a pile of laundry dumped at the bottom of the stairs, waiting to be taken up, or a box of toys oddly placed on a desk in the study.

KITCHEN CHAOS In the kitchen, you would expect to see either an abundance of food spilling out everywhere or no food at all. As a visitor, making a cup of tea will be a real effort, since you have to hunt for tea bags and sugar; they seem to be hidden away and out of reach. You may also find that the cupboards are empty of good quality ingredients that could be used to cool a nourishing meal.

Organize your family's belongings so that everything has its appropriate place.

FLOORS Earth energy is about our ability to contact the earth, and floor coverings often hold clues to its state of balance. Houses where the occupants haven't got around to laying floors or use inappropriate substitutes often suffer from an imbalance of earth energy. I once did a consultation in a house where the floors had been lined with a furnishing fabric (white calico), not a flooring material. No wonder its occupants felt unsettled!

Make sure your color schemes reflect your natural surroundings.

DECOR Another strong indication that earth energy is unbalanced is when color schemes have gone askew; for example, a light blue floor with terra-cotta walls and ceiling will give the room's inhabitants the feeling that they've been turned upside down! Once you start thinking in terms of the earth, this becomes very obvious stuff.

how to remedy earth energy

It is always worth taking the time to remedy your earth energy, because you will find that when it is in balance, you will really improve your ability to maintain a successful relationship, whether it is with a live-in lover, family, friends, or colleagues, enriching your life all around.

Earth energy has a pulling power that encourages our gardening instincts.

CREATE BOUNDARIES First, make the boundaries of your living space clear. If you can't put physical boundaries around your property, walk the boundary every day. A lot of people do this instinctively; on fine evenings, many couples stroll around the edge of their garden looking at the plants. They may not even question why they have this inclination, but it is their natural instinct to set out the boundaries and remedy earth energy asserting itself.

STAY GROUNDED We discharge energy into the ground and draw nourishment back up from the earth. To do this effectively, we need to be grounded through natural substances rather than energy-depleting synthetic materials, so another way to remedy earth energy is to purchase natural floor coverings such as seagrass. Allow the universe to supply all the nourishment you need to live a fulfilled and active life, and you will be able to throw away those vitamins!

Natural floor coverings such as earth-baked terra-cotta help us to stay grounded.

BE VIGILANT Don't get too rigid, but do try to keep things in their appropriate places. Don't brush your teeth at the kitchen sink; do it in the bathroom. Stop the overspill between rooms. Also, try to avoid introducing imbalances. Match the single armchair in your living room with a similarly sized one, not a footstool. There's room for bigger and smaller in your home, but not for huge and tiny. Remember at all times: balance, balance, balance!

spoiling yourself!

In remedying your earth energy, the message to send to yourself is that life is easily available to you. Remember, you're wonderful exactly as you are, and you should set up your environment so that it constantly feeds that message back to you.

TREAT YOURSELF Buy the best quality cookies you can afford, rather than five bargain packages of cheap ones. Make sure you have somewhere nice to sit within your home, and find a place inside it that will inspire you, like a window with a beautiful view.

PLAN YOUR TIME Allow yourself to get into a natural rhythm, by allowing yourself adequate time to complete the tasks you have to do. If you always find yourself rushing around in the morning when you're trying to get ready for work, you're placing a great deal of pressure on yourself and setting every day off to a stressful start! Arrange your living space to make life as easy as possible for yourself. Clear some space, put up some hooks or a rail to store your work clothes, and get them out the night before, so they are easily available in the morning and you don't waste time delving into wardrobes and drawers trying to find a clean shirt or blouse or matching socks.

Arrange your life to avoid undue stress. For instance, you could organize your clothes so that things are easy to find.

MAKE FOOD A PLEASURE Don't store beans and legumes in jars when you know you only have 20 minutes available for cooking every night. It's better to buy salads, cheese, and good quality bread, which will make a nourishing meal quickly. Pull the things you use frequently, such as tea bags, to the front of the cupboard, so that you don't have to keep rooting behind other jars and containers for them. Don't make food inaccessible and hard to find.

Be realistic about the time you usually have available for preparing food. Don't store anything you won't use.

OBSERVE THE SEASONS Also, try to get in tune with seasonal changes. Although it is part of the natural cycle of our lives, some people find it very hard to cope with the dark, cold days of winter. If this is the case with you, consider what you could give yourself to make winter more enjoyable. Spend money on a good wood-burning stove, so that you can snuggle up in front of it on cold days. You need to experience winter, as it is the water part of the cycle, but a short vacation somewhere sunny and warm can do you a world of good.

If you get depressed by the onset of dark winter days, a vacation in the sun might be the answer.

happy to be single?

If you are not currently in a relationship, but think you would like to be, look around your own space to find out how you stand and use your observations to diagnose what is going on in your life. Does your house have an imbalance of chi? Does it create a very strong statement that says, "Being single is fine by me!"? Where do you stand right now, and where do you want to be?

THE HAPPY HOME When you visit the house of a single person who is happy to live alone, you will often find one beautiful, healthy tree in the garden, one comfortable armchair in the living room (often alongside a rather harder seat), one stool at the breakfast bar in the kitchen, and a luxurious bathroom obviously set up for one person, with one towel on the rail. In the bedroom, the bed is often pushed up against the wall, so that only one person can get into it easily.

Is your home only suitable for a single person? If this is not what you want, take steps to change your environment.

THE LONELY HOME I have done so many consultations where the client says, "I'd really like to have a partner." But when I look around his home, I realize he actually hasn't created the space for anybody else to live there, because the house is chock full of his possessions. He may even have to clear books and magazines off a chair before I can sit down!

FILL THE GAPS If you recognize your own space in the above two descriptions, you should ask yourself why you give out such a strong message to the universe that you are happily single, if you do in fact feel a relationship would make your life complete? Perhaps a relationship isn't what you need; maybe you are unfulfilled in some other way and think you need a relationship to fill that gap. If someone has a very low sense of self-worth despite being very successful in a career, that person might feel the need for a relationship to feel more supported, when there may in fact be other ways of increasing self-esteem.

The single life might suit you, so don't look for a partner just to conform to social expectations.

PUT OUT THE WELCOME MAT If, however, you still feel that you need a partner to feel completely fulfilled, make that theoretical person welcome in your home. Take measures like adding a second armchair or another chair in the kitchen and clear some space so that there is room for someone to enter your life. Prepare your home to accommodate a couple.

If you have set up your home for one person, perhaps you should think again about whether you want a partner.

when things go stale

In my work as a Feng Shui practitioner, it's not just single people who want to consult me about their love lives. Even when a long-term couple seem ideally suited, there can often be deep-rooted problems under the superficial appearance of happiness.

Feng Shui offers practical help for emotional problems in relationships.

IDENTIFY THE PROBLEM Sometimes when a couple have been together a long time, they find their relationship has gone stale, although they can't put their finger on anything specific that has gone wrong. Feng Shui can help you to pinpoint and remedy the problem, even when you don't know what to do in emotional terms, because it lets you work things out at a physical level.

SIGNS AND SYMPTOMS As a Feng Shui consultant, when I walk into a house, I don't need to be told if there are problems within the relationship. The front of the house, reception rooms, and hallways may be beautiful, but when I walk into the garden and look back at the

house, I find it shabby, with broken guttering, moldy walls, broken paths, or dying plants. If I open the door of a room that guests aren't supposed to enter or delve into out-of-the-way cupboards, I find lots of dull, outdated objects that no longer apply to the couple's lives. They might even have a junk room, crammed with old items that they don't use anymore. This all signals to me that, even if on the surface they appear to be the perfect couple, when you looked at the underside of the relationship, you see neglect and things that should not have been ignored. By identifying areas of neglect in your home, you can start to repair your relationship by ignoring the superficial and paying attention to the underlying qualities of your partner.

Junk often indicates a failure to move on from the past.

Check the back of your house for signs of neglect, and take action to remedy it.

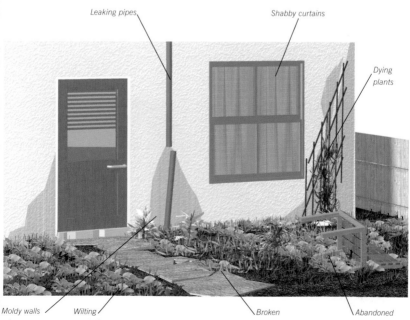

Leaking pipes

Shabby curtains

Dying plants

Moldy walls

Wilting vegetation

Broken pathway

Abandoned furniture

81

reviving a relationship

When you are trying to remedy the problems in a long-term relationship, it's important to go back to the roots of the situation, and that can mean that you need to practice Feng Shui at a very basic level within your home environment.

Keep your bedroom tidy to maintain the right energy levels in a close relationship.

TIDY UP Walk into your backyard, study the back of your house for signs of neglect, and think of ways in which you can make the view more interesting; you will find some very direct symbols there of what's going wrong in your relationship. Tidy up those forgotten, out-of-the-way cupboards, and if you find in them—or in the spare room or even your bedroom—objects that you haven't used in years, you can see that it really is ultimately a matter of neglect; you simply haven't been paying sufficient attention to the relationship.

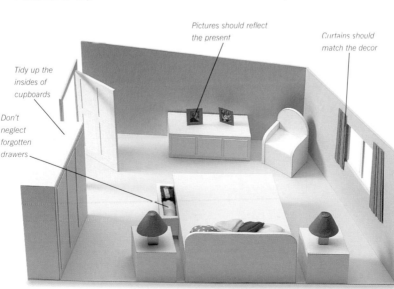

Pictures should reflect the present

Curtains should match the decor

Tidy up the insides of cupboards

Don't neglect forgotten drawers

ATTEND TO DETAILS Start to devote as much care to the less obvious, hidden areas of your home as you do to the main rooms. While you put fresh flowers into the spare bedroom in your living space, plan something exciting, like an exotic vacation, with your partner. Spend more time together, one to one. Indulge in a romantic dinner for two instead of going out with a group of friends. Even if the evening isn't ideal, you'll understand why it's gone wrong and you can start to address the underlying problems, rather than, as it were, living all the time on show in the reception rooms of your house, under the public gaze of your friends.

Though "quality time" may sound like a cliché, it strengthens our emotional bonds.

CASE STUDY

I once did a consultation where a wife called me in because her husband had lost all interest in her and she suspected he was having an affair. The house was large, and the master bedroom had two dressing rooms and a master bathroom. She had decorated the room in a very frilly, feminine style, and both dressing rooms and the bathroom were full of her clothes and toiletries. The husband had to keep his clothes in the downstairs cloakroom and wasn't allowed to use the master bathroom! I pointed out to her that she'd created a huge imbalance, effectively pushing him out of the bedroom, and instead of fighting his way back in, he'd given up the struggle and taken a mistress instead. My advice was to clear out one of the dressing rooms for him and let him use the bathroom—that's the route back to the bedroom!

a state of balance

There are no magical solutions when you are suffering from relationship problems, but by using Feng Shui to correct imbalances in your earth energy, you can learn to identify them and work toward putting them right.

INVESTIGATE YOUR ENERGY First, look around your home and ask yourself the appropriate questions, so that you can ascertain what is going on in your life. Then look at the ways in which your earth energy is out of balance and think of how you can remedy it.

KEEP OBSERVING If you make these questions part of an ongoing process, you will find yourself feeling more centered and rooted. This, in turn, will lead to you becoming a healthier person, physically, mentally, and spiritually, enabling you to blossom. You will find that the things you need will then come to you, as you

Grounding yourself with earth energy can bring positive changes into your working life.

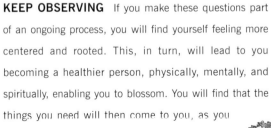

find yourself to be in the right place at the right time for meeting, not just a mate, but also some new friends, or perhaps winning a new job. Earth energy is so important to our overall well-being that, even if we did nothing else with Feng Shui but clutter-clearing and working to balance our earth energy, life would undoubtedly take a turn for the better.

MAINTAIN A BALANCE Other people will instinctively recognize when your earth energy is in balance and will become attracted to you, because they can sense that you have your life sorted out. Equally, when you have balanced your earth energy, there is also a much better chance that you will attract a mate whose earth energy is in a similar state of balance.

To return to my earlier flower analogy, if you are a beautiful bloom that has no roots, you are likely to attract a butterfly type of personality, who is only interested in the flower. However, when the flower wilts, because the roots are unhealthy, the butterfly moves on to another bloom. If you are in balance, you will attract someone in a similar situation, which is the best possible result. When two people whose earth energy is in balance get together, maintaining the relationship will not be a struggle but will instead become part of the natural cycle of life.

You can only attract a suitable partner if you give out the right energy signals.

QUICK FIXES

1. It's hard to suggest quick fixes for love and romance, because they are about earth energy, it's a long-term cyclical process. It is about the whole cycle of seasons, so there are no fast solutions.

2. The best thing to do is to take an overview of your life and ascertain where you are in your cycle here and now, at the moment.

3. Are you currently in the winter phase? Then rest up and prepare yourself for the spring.

4. Are you in a summer period? Get out and party! The best way to start correcting your level of energy is to know yourself and find out what you need.

family harmony

Obviously, Feng Shui is practiced within the boundaries of your own house and yard. But did you know that you should start to employ Feng Shui before you even move in, while you are still looking for a new home? And once you've found the house of your dreams, it can help you to resolve a wide variety of family problems, ranging from a sleepless baby to an untidy teenager.

house-hunting
with feng shui

Achieving family harmony involves creating

a balance between active and passive chi within

your home—and this is a process that should start before you even

move into a new house, while you are still

looking for a suitable property.

If you are finding it hard to settle into a new home, you may look for reasons to stay out of the house.

QUESTIONS TO ASK YOURSELF

1. Do you know why the people who lived in your house before you moved out?

2. Has your family found it hard to "settle" since you've moved into your new home?

3. Do you have a disruptive child living in the house with you?

4. Do you find yourself constantly nagging your teenager to tidy up his or her room?

5. Does your baby continually disturb you by refusing to sleep through the night?

HOUSE HISTORY While you are house-hunting, you should be looking for a home that will be both supportive and nurturing to your family. When you find a property that meets your physical requirements, ask the realtor or the present occupants why they are moving out—and also if they know why the people before them moved out. Don't be surprised if they get very uncomfortable about answering this question; this is because they are subconsciously aware of how meaningful their answer will be. If they won't tell you and you can't find out, assume that it's for a negative reason rather than the more positive reasons of moving in with a new partner, starting a family, or winning a job promotion, which involves a new location.

INHERITED ENERGY Houses have a tendency to repeat their histories. For example, if a property has become available because the present occupants are a couple who are about to split up and go their separate ways, it is part of a pattern that the subsequent inhabitants are likely to follow, so that any later occupants who are involved in a relationship are also likely to divorce while they are living there.

A house can retain energy from its previous occupants. Look for signs of imbalance before you buy a new property.

SEE THE SIGNS A good Feng Shui consultant should be able to walk into the house and quickly pinpoint the reason why a relationship came to an end, or why someone lost a job. Hopefully, when you've become familiar with the recommendations in this book, you'll also be able to look at a building and spot signals that will tell you what event led the present occupants to move out.

stopping history
from repeating itself

Because houses repeat their histories, before you move into a new home, it's important to try to learn as much about its previous occupants, and their reasons for moving out, as you can.

Look for the reasons behind the "For Sale" sign—they may be very enlightening.

BUYER BEWARE! Hazardous houses to watch out for are those that are becoming vacant as a result of divorce, unemployment, financial problems, death (if this was not due to the ending of a natural cycle, as in old age), illness, or disablement caused by an accident. It's also not a good sign if it is the only house on the road that has changed hands frequently in the last few years, when the rest of the street has been occupied by the same families for a long time. (If the current owner knows why the last two or three occupants moved out, it has probably had several within a short space of time.) This awareness has nothing to do with the intuitions you feel when you walk into a house; it has to do with concrete facts.

REMEDY BAD CHI If the house does have an unhappy history, it doesn't necessarily mean that you shouldn't move in, because it is possible to remedy difficult chi. The most important weapon that you have in your armory is an awareness of what's wrong with the building. If someone has moved out because they ran out of money, you may observe that the surrounding area is sloping away from the house, symbolizing the draining of wealth from the property. If that's the case, you can build a wall to stop prosperity from trickling away. Or you may realize that the huge tree that overshadows the front garden is preventing new opportunities from entering the house and see the need to cut it down.

If previous occupants suffered from money troubles, keep an eye on your own finances for twelve months after moving in.

reverting to type

Ornaments alter the energy of a house, but disappear when the occupants move out.

The way the energy works in a house won't change fundamentally unless you consciously decide to alter it by using Feng Shui. However, it is sometimes possible for people unaware of Feng Shui practice to make subconscious corrections to houses, which may work as well as if they were intentional.

TEMPORARY REMEDIES When people move out, they often take their house improvements with them. The house then reverts back to its earlier type of energy and can repeat its history from before they moved in. Sometimes, while house-hunting, you may come across a building that shows classic signs of imbalance—just the kind of house where you'd expect to find a couple on the verge of splitting up. However, if the partners moving out are still happily together, be aware that they may have, consciously or unconsciously, remedied their home's energy deficiencies with furnishings or decor. The problem is that when they move out, they take away the big red picture that was hanging in the hall, helping healthy chi to circulate around the house, or they remove the big statue from the garden where it was supporting the wealth area, or they pull up the Persian rugs that were remedying the earth energy. So when you move into an empty house, things then start to go wrong.

GOOD OBSERVATION If you see signs of imbalance within a house, but the people who were previously living in it appear to be happy together, make a mental note of the key objects that they are taking away with them. You may even find that part of your attraction to the house was due to the fixtures and fittings that they are removing; in other words, you are subconsciously keying in to the remedies they chose. So if you find yourself admiring their rug, be aware that if you follow them into the house and don't buy a similar one, you may start to experience some problems.

The seller's soft furnishings, fixtures, and fittings often subconsciously attract you to a property.

REVERTING TO TYPE

I was once asked to look at a house purchased by a divorcee. The woman who'd owned it before her had just acquired a new job and was moving out to live with her new partner. The divorcee hoped that she would inherit some of the history of the house, and that as a result, something similar would happen to her when she moved into the property. However, she decided that she wanted to make some very drastic structural changes to the building—changes that would have altered the dynamic of the house completely. When she called me in for a consultation, I had to advise her to moderate her restructuring plans, because it would have opened up the house too much, speeding up the flow of chi. I've since found out that she followed my advice, and that her life has been very happy and successful since moving in.

The harmony of a new home will rely on the appropriate placement of your own furniture and ornaments.

93

atmosphere and energy

When you see a property you like the look of, you may think that you've found your ideal home. However, if it just doesn't feel "right" after you've moved in, it may need a good space-clearing to remove the remaining energy of its previous occupants.

TEETHING PROBLEMS Sometimes when you move into a house, you pick up a strange vibe in the place. The layout is great, the number of rooms is just right for you, and they're all well-sited with a south-facing reception room and a north-facing bathroom. On paper, the house fulfills everything you wanted from it. You do a comprehensive Feng Shui check, and it passes with flying colors. However, the atmosphere inside the building just doesn't feel right. After you've moved in, the children start bickering, the baby stops sleeping through the night, the dog becomes increasingly restless and barks continually, the cat urinates everywhere—yet your logical reasoning and intuitive feelings are telling you that this is definitely the house for you.

Good instincts about a property may be confounded by the erratic behavior of the family after moving in.

ENERGETIC IMPRINTS The problem could be an imprint that's been left on the house by past events that have taken place within it, and it might just need to be cleared out. Energetic imprints are things that you can't see or analyze. They're not covered in the Ancient Chinese philosophy about types of chi, and they don't fit into any structural model, but nevertheless, if you've experienced them, you will be very aware that they exist. They have tangible effects on the atmosphere of a house.

PHYSICAL SYMPTOMS   There are a number of indications that a house needs space-clearing. For example, if it's constantly getting untidy and you don't understand why, because you've got adequate space, time, help, and motivation to keep it organized. Other signals include light bulbs that keep burning out and computers that persist in crashing, despite being used correctly. Leaks may occur that can't be explained by plumbers, or cracks will inexplicably appear in walls or crockery or glass. Your dog may refuse to settle, but will insist on running around and barking, and the house and its grounds may suffer from infestations of ants, wasps, and other insects. You may also find that flowers tend to die more quickly inside its rooms, rosebuds never come into bloom, and tulips wilt instantly. Generally, a bad, fractious atmosphere will extend throughout the house.

EMOTIONAL SYMPTOMS   Children are far more sensitive than adults to this kind of thing, and can act as an energy barometer. They may start to display symptoms such as underachieving at school, disturbances in their sleep patterns, eczema, asthma, and/or rhinitis, or become whiny and clinging, while teenagers will find any number of excuses to stay out of the house. Obviously, many different things can cause this kind of behavior, but one reason could be the urgent need to space-clear your home.

Cracked glass is not only unhygienic—it also signals a need for space-clearing.

Bad behavior in your children could simply be a sign of stagnant energy in the home.

space-clearing

Space-clearing can have very beneficial effects on the atmosphere of your home, but there is nothing mystical about the technique. It is a very easy, straightforward practice, and is something that everyone can learn to do at its most basic level.

Candles will clear the atmosphere, and a vase of fresh flowers will energize your living space.

DO IT YOURSELF There are two kinds of space-clearing. The first can be done by anyone for himself if he knows how, and this is the kind I will explain fully here. It will sort out the atmosphere in a house where bad things have happened or where people simply haven't cleared out their junk for a long time. It works well where houses have got clogged up, sad, and tired, and where the occupants are bored and can't think straight.

THE SPACE-CLEARING RITUAL In its most basic form, there is a ritual you can follow whenever you move into a house. Place a lighted candle, a vase of fresh flowers, or a bowl of salt inside every room of your new home. The candle represents enlightenment and will clean out the atmosphere (please remember that you must never leave a lighted candle unattended). Flowers symbolize new growth and will enliven the atmosphere. Salt will remove negativity and place your own imprint on the space; you can either put a pile of it in the middle of the room or scatter it around the perimeter.

When you have placed one of these objects in each of the rooms, leave them there for a predetermined time. This can be as long or as short as you decide to make it,

whether it is 60 minutes, 24 hours, or a week. At the end of that time, the candles, flowers, and salt should be thrown away and removed to outside the boundary of the house. Remember that items you use for any kind of space-clearing should never be reused for another purpose. If you keep special objects in the home specifically for space-clearing, store them wrapped in silk up on a shelf rather than at ground level.

The refining force of fire can remedy any negative energy patterns in a room.

CALL IN AN EXPERT The second type of space-clearing can be employed where there have been more serious problems, such as long-term illness or an untimely death. I have even been called in to clear the space where a house has burned down. For this kind of space clearing, all I can advise you to do is to call in an expert, because you must really know what you're doing before you begin.

Salt will absorb any negative vibrations from the past history of a house.

preparing to space-clear

If you decide to space-clear your home thoroughly, you should think of it as undertaking some really high quality housework. You are going to go into every single corner of the house with the feeling of care and love and the intention of creating harmony.

FOCUS YOUR MIND The feeling and intention are both really important, so before you start to space-clear, focus your mind on what your aim is. There is no point in space-clearing unless you are very sure about the outcome you want to achieve.

CONFIRM YOUR INTENTIONS It's best to keep the intention really broad; if you wish to bring happiness to a specific child, it may be at the expense of others, so a better aim might be to establish harmony or well-being within the house. You can even take a clean sheet of

Direct your good intentions to the whole family rather than just one member.

paper, write the intention down, date the paper, sign it, and then leave it at the starting point for your space-clearing—preferably with something that symbolizes what you are trying to achieve, like a beautiful five-petaled flower to represent harmony, a lighted candle for clarity, or a bowl of water to symbolize calm.

Candles bring clarity to the energy of a room, and will help you to focus on the task of clearing.

DESIGNATE AN AREA   When you space-clear, you will need to move around as much of the space as you feel you can cope with at any one time. Limit yourself to a particular area that you feel you can tackle in the time allowed, whether it is simply the pathway to the house or the entire ground floor or the garden. Keep it realistic and don't get overambitious; only you know how much time you have at your disposal.

A five-petaled flower symbolizes the harmony you aspire to in the family home.

CLEAR THE SPACE   As you start to space-clear, move into that area consciously. The idea is to travel all the way through the space physically, using your body to clear it, always keeping in your mind and your heart what you're trying to do. Don't rush around, but move at the pace you feel the space needs you to move at. Sometimes you may feel the need to move quickly, sometimes you may need to stand still. Sometimes you may need to skip, sometimes you may need to tread very carefully. Be as sensitive to the space as you would be to the moods of a person, and ask yourself, with every step, what that part of the space needs.

how to space-clear

When you first start to space-clear, you may feel nothing at all—except slightly ridiculous! But if you take the process seriously and trust that it works, you will find that as you travel around the space, you will sense what is needed to change the atmosphere.

Follow your intuition when choosing the tools you will use for space-clearing.

SENSE THE MOOD You might think one corner needs livening up, since it seems gloomy, so you could sing a snatch of a song there, if you like singing, or whistle, or clap your hands, or you may want to bring it a gift in the form of a red flower. You may feel that another part of a room needs calming down, so you might decide to sit down there quietly for a few minutes, and when you move on, you could leave a pile of sand to earth the space.

CORRECT THE ENERGY As you travel around the area you have chosen, don't simply be aware of the space at eye level; also look at the space above and below it, so that none of it is neglected. If you feel the space at the top of the room is dank and stale, throw a handful of salt or sand into it, or wave a ribbon in it, to liven it up. If the ground doesn't feel substantial, scatter sand onto it or place something heavy on it, like a pair of walking boots or a stone, to anchor it.

CLOSE THE RITUAL When you've reached the end of your circuit, return to your starting point, sit down, and ask yourself if you've now finished or whether you need to return to any area, if there is any space that you've missed, if things have cleared to a certain degree and now the next layer has revealed itself—because sometimes space-clearing needs to be done layer by layer. However, if you don't have the time or the energy to tackle any more at that moment, make a mental note of what still needs to be done and make an appointment with yourself for doing it. Alternatively, if you don't feel up to doing any more space-clearing for a while, ask the universe to do the rest for you. Don't overload yourself, because you should never get yourself into a position in which you feel out of your depth and uncomfortable.

If a particular room seems overwhelming, it may be best to call in an expert.

problem children

It's sometimes surprising how much of an effect the placement of rooms within the home can have on the family who occupy it. Often the problems exhibited by young children can be remedied by changing their rooms to make them feel more secure within the family.

PLACEMENT Once you've moved into your new home and done your space-clearing, you'll start looking at who's going to have which room. Placement—that is, where people are placed physically within the house—is very important, because it can be used as an effective Feng Shui cure when you've just moved into a new dwelling or when family members are showing symptoms that they're not coping well with living in your current one.

PROBLEMS WITH ANGER Children don't have many ways of showing anger. But if they refuse to wear the clothes you buy them, constantly get toys out but don't actually play with them, or sulk when they're called in from outside for dinner and refuse to eat—basically, they are displaying classic signs of anger. They, of course, don't usually know what's wrong with them, and nine times out of ten, simply giving them more love and attention will help to put things right. But this doesn't mean buying yet more clothes or cooking a variety of different tempting dishes at every mealtime. It can be about pulling them deeper into your life and being prepared to share more of yourself with them.

Keep an eye out for anger in your child, and remedy it with love and attention.

A FENG SHUI SOLUTION Feng Shui can draw a child's energy closer to you. If your child is displaying any signs of unhappiness, look at where his or her bedroom is situated. If it's at the end of a corridor, in an extension, or on the opposite side of the house to your own, you are effectively banishing the child to the outskirts of family life, so move him or her into the bedroom that's closest to your room. You should especially avoid having a bathroom or the baby's room between your room and that of another child, even if it means moving the baby's crib into your bedroom. If you have to have a bedroom in an extension, keep it for guests—or give it to a teenager or young adult who is preparing to move out, so that it becomes a kind of halfway house for him as he is learning to spread his wings.

The floor plan above shuts the older child out of the family unit.

Teenagers' bedrooms can be placed away from the master bedroom, allowing them to express their individuality.

placement for contentment

There are a number of important considerations you should bear in mind when it comes to the placement of your own and your children's bedrooms, to ensure that they feel loved, stable, and completely secure within the family home.

Feelings of insecurity are unavoidable if a door opens onto the top of the stairs.

THE MASTER BEDROOM Choose the location of the main bedroom, in relation to the other bedrooms, very carefully. Make sure it is in the most powerful area of the house. Don't imagine that you will be doing your children a favor if you give them the best bedroom. This will disturb the balance within the family, since they will become the most powerful people in the household, while their parents, who should be responsible for them as they grow up, won't have the energy to do the job properly. Consequently, the children will thrive, but become disobedient and unruly, while their parents become depleted and exhausted. So don't imagine you're being selfish by choosing the best bedroom for yourself!

CHILDREN'S ROOMS Try to avoid putting a child in a bedroom at the top of the stairs. This sets up an unsafe dynamic—particularly for a baby, because the insecurity of its position will prevent it from sleeping through the night. Babies need to be nurtured in the heart of the household, not near the stairs, in a bay window, or in an extension.

PLAYROOMS If your children have become clingy or constantly interrupt you when they should be absorbed in playing together, look at the location of their playroom. A playroom in an extension will never be effective unless an adult is with the children while they are inside it. The playroom needs to be near the kitchen or a room where other family members spend their time. Children want to be included in day-to-day living, and if they're not in close proximity to them, they will repeatedly come in and ask for attention, often in the guise of requests for drinks or snacks. If you are nearby, they won't need to ask.

If you don't have enough space for a playroom, keep an area of the kitchen free where the children can play while you get on with your chores. Bring your children into your life—within certain boundaries—rather than leaving them on the periphery, and the whole family will be happier.

Remember that energy comes from living beings rather than plastic toys.

Make your children feel part of your life by allowing them to share your space.

Give space to your children's toys

leave room on the kitchen table for drawing

diagnosing the root cause of family problems

Sometimes the cause of a problem within the home is not immediately obvious and will require deeper insights to identify it. You will then need to take your time and employ a greater degree of awareness to ascertain what is wrong.

HIDDEN ANXIETIES When I go to see a house, very often what appears to be the problem with the house is just the symptom of the real problem. For example, if I visit a family home, where the consultation is about the fact that the father or mother doesn't have enough time to spend with the children, the problem may manifest itself by the children frequently falling ill, so that somebody has to take time off work to look after them. In a house with this kind of problem, you will often see a lot of dull colors, tired furnishings, faded patterns on fabrics, general muddle, and objects that are out of place. These are the symptoms, but the actual cause is that the parent is frequently absent.

The absence of a well-loved parent can have far-reaching negative effects on family life.

LOOK FOR CLUES If you're viewing the situation with Feng Shui eyes, you need to look beyond the symptom to the cause, so you need to seek out things that may be less obvious. The way you can diagnose this for yourself is to work out where you habitually stand in a room

when you are talking to somebody about that particular problem, because that place indicates the root cause of it. So, if you customarily stand with your back to the window while you're talking about the problem, turn around and look out of the window. If you see a broken path or gate or a pile of rubble or a dead bush, that could be where the problem lies. As a consultant, I often find it lies in the part of the house that the occupants forget to show me as we walk around their home, or sometimes I can ascertain it from where they stand within a room.

The view out of the window can often give clues to the source of a persistent problem.

GOOD FENG SHUI So remember to look beyond the superficial. The person displaying the symptoms of the problem is not usually its root cause. That is the mark of good Feng Shui: not rushing to remedy the obvious, but taking time to work out the real problem.

different rooms for different people

There is no such thing as a "good" or "bad" Feng Shui room. Every room has something to offer someone—with the possible exception of a room without a window, which I personally don't think is fit for human habitation at all! Even rooms that classical Feng Shui theory would say are completely negative will serve a purpose.

Even rooms with negative Feng Shui characteristics can have beneficial effects on the right person.

MAKE USE OF "NEGATIVE" ENERGY Take the scenario of a bedroom with a sloping ceiling. Many Feng Shui practitioners would consider this to be a very inauspicious room, because the sloping ceiling cuts through the heaven energy, disrupting the balance between earth energy and heaven energy. This would boost fire energy which is active, and would not make for restful surroundings. However, for someone who is very firmly stuck in a rut, this room might prove beneficial, at least temporarily. The excess of fire energy would be a shock to

A sloping ceiling is very inauspicious

This bathroom will drain energy away

their system, and might even make them feel slightly ill, but it would jolt them out of their rut. Similarly a bedroom situated over a garage, resulting in a lack of grounding, might be helpful to someone who needed to get away from the present for a while and find a vision for the future.

Large windows in bedrooms need soft drapes to slow the flow of chi and create a calm atmosphere.

ROOMS WITH A PURPOSE You will gradually sense how to use different rooms to achieve different results. An energizing south-facing room with a bay window may be fine as a playroom for a schoolchild, as long as he or she has a more relaxing bedroom. Even a room full of clutter can serve a purpose. You should never order someone to clear his room, because it may be helping him by slowing him down. If it slows him down so far that he eventually gets stuck, perhaps it will force him to take action. If you keep removing clutter, you are only prolonging the situation.

Busy, colorful surroundings are conducive to activity and play.

adolescent angst

Adolescence can be a very difficult time of life for a child. Whether your child is moody and withdrawn or noisy and out of control, Feng Shui can help to introduce a greater degree of balance, and consequently contentment, into his or her life.

UNDERSTAND THE SYMPTOMS The important thing about Feng Shui is to understand other people's processes and to know when to interfere and when to stand back and let things take their course. That's not to say that you should give your children free rein and let them pile up clutter in the middle of their room, but try to understand what they are doing and why.

OBSESSION WITH BLACK If your teenager starts to paint everything in his room black and to surround himself with floor-to-ceiling units covered in black stereo equipment, understand that he is trying to absorb energy and slow things down. He is struggling to get into water/winter energy, because the changes in his life are too much for him to cope with. Instead of going into his room with an ultimatum: "That's it—you've got to clear this out!", you should ask him, "Is life really tricky at the moment? What can we do to help? Do you want to get together with some friends? Would you like a lift into town?" By helping him out of that winter phase, you may find that he comes back to you and announces that he wants to get rid of his black sofa or repaint his room in brighter colors.

An obsession with black can indicate an inability to keep up with change.

MINIMALISM   Similarly, if your teenager is becoming increasingly minimalist and is excluding more and more things from her life, while painting her bedroom white, understand that she is struggling to control the events in her life. In this case, the conversation should run along the lines of: "Do you feel that things are getting on top of you? What support do you need?" You may then find that she starts adding things to the room.

UNTIDINESS   An untidy adolescent may be signaling that he is overwhelmed and can't cope by physically demonstrating the chaos that surrounds him in terms of clutter. If you order him to tidy his room, you are piling more pressure on him; asking him, "Are you doing too many activities? Would you like to give up some of them?" may create a better result. Try to understand your teenager and support him in his change, rather than attempting to make the change for him.

Minimalism can indicate exhaustion and a need to control one's surroundings.

Plain white walls with no pictures

Lack of clutter

babies and young children

Babies and young children need safe, calm rooms. Try to create a peaceful environment; they don't need extra stimulation, because they get more than enough from life in general. Most importantly, remember to consider the room from the child's perspective.

Moderation is the key when introducing colorful objects into young children's rooms.

DECOR Keep young children's rooms clutter-free, decorated in gentle pastel colors, and full of soft, flowing shapes and calming images. Have a couple of items hanging high up, so that they do look upward from time to time, but keep most things at a low level. Children don't need a ceiling covered in mobiles or a frieze that goes around the room at an adult's eye level. A frieze should be at the eye level of your child, or, even better, at heart level, because this is where you want them to operate from, rather than their head.

FURNITURE You can rely on your baby or young child to develop fantastically on its own, but remember my flower analogy from the Basics section and the importance of supporting its roots while it's growing. Keep babies' cribs away from sloping ceilings. Keep bed heads away from windows, where your child will not feel supported, or line bed ends up with the door. Walk around the room, imagining you were feeling very unsettled, and see where you would choose to sleep, or work out the place where a dog would instinctively curl up. That's where you could place the crib. Follow your instincts. Try imagining what you would see if you were lying in it yourself; when we put a crib in place, we very often stand back from it and look at the baby, when of course the baby's experience is the other way around.

SOFT TOYS Some children's bedrooms contain rows of soft toys. People buy these because they want to be loved, so they buy something they want for themselves and give it to your baby! Your child only needs two or so soft toys to choose from; otherwise, because she is overwhelmed by the variety, she may reject them and won't use anything for comfort. You don't need to surround your baby with everyone else's desire to be loved!

A bedroom that is too cluttered and busy can be confusing and overstimulating for a small child.

Avoid complicating the ceiling with too many hanging objects

Try not to confuse your child with too large a variety of toys

Keep cribs away from sloping ceilings and windows

113

QUICK FIXES

1. Sweep the path in from the gate to the front of the house and out at the back of the house.

2. Doing your housework thoroughly, including things like hanging rugs outside, shaking curtains out, and airing duvets, is as good as space-clearing, especially if you do it with the intention of "out with the old and in with the new."

3. Help your children by setting a good example. If they see you clearing out clutter and enjoying it, they will start to do it themselves. If they see you holding on to things, they'll do the same thing.

4. Don't fill your children's rooms with the toys that would have made your childhood ideal. You are simply trying to fill up your own empty spaces.

5. Put a comfy rug on the floor of your children's bedroom to encourage them to sprawl on the floor. It's good for their physical growth and keeps them stay well grounded.

health

We cannot live our lives to the fullest if we do not enjoy good health. Yet how many of us are guilty of running our bodies into the ground with the excessive demands we place on them? By using Feng Shui in our living space, we can improve our health, not only in terms of avoiding major illnesses, but also in terms of eradicating those annoying sniffles and allergies that can dog our everyday lives.

taking care of yourself

The importance of good health is widely recognized in society today. Yet, ironically, people are probably putting more demands on their health than ever before. Most of us expect too much from our bodies, demanding that they perform at a constant level, whatever punishment we decide to put them through.

QUESTIONS TO ASK YOURSELF

1. How do you define health?

2. Is what you expect from your body appropriate for your age, the time of year, your level of activity, emotional situation, and position in life?

3. Do you expect to be free from all ailments that would disrupt your day-to-day routine, including minor ones?

4. Do you expect to have endless amounts of energy and vitality?

5. Do you see your body as a resource that you can endlessly plunder without taking time to support it?

Today's world is obsessed by fitness, and often confuses physical strength and stamina with general good health.

RESPECT YOURSELF Enjoying good health is about having realistic expectations and treating your body with respect. There's no point in downing vitamins and energy-boosting drinks when what your body really needs is adequate rest in a stress-free environment and a good, balanced diet. Take notice when you feel discomfort—it's your body's way of telling you to slow down.

OBSERVE YOUR HABITS You can work out what you expect from your body from how you are using the space immediately around you right now. Take a few minutes to consider how you are currently positioning yourself. Have you taken care of yourself in the way you've set yourself up, or have you just sat down without thinking in a position that somebody else has gestured you toward? Or perhaps you simply feel too rushed to consider how you've organized yourself in the here and now?

Good posture and comfort are vital to the effective functioning of the physical body.

CHECK YOUR SURROUNDINGS Look around. What can you see from where you are sitting? Is what you have given yourself to look at nurturing and inspiring? Will it allow you to experience an uncluttered, clear train of thought? Look behind you. Have you positioned yourself with support at your back, or is there a lot of activity going on behind you, which will make you feel constantly anxious and pressured, even while you think you are ignoring it?

SUPPORT YOUR BODY Look to your right and left. Have you situated yourself with a good degree of protection, or is something looming over you and casting a shadow? Have you given yourself adequate room, or have you squeezed yourself into a gap that you consider is appropriate for what other people demand from you?

By reading through this section, you can learn how to take responsibility for your health on a really basic level and how to become more conscious of how you can support your body.

choosing what's appropriate

Although we all know the basic rules about good diet, adequate sleep, and so on, it's important to acknowledge that our bodies' needs are constantly changing. As a consequence, we need to constantly reassess the amount and type of nourishment we need.

When we do more than one thing at a time it is very easy to strain our body with bad posture.

FIND YOUR SPACE

Carrying on from the exercise described on the previous pages, consider whether the room you are sitting in is appropriate to your current needs. In choosing it, did you acknowledge whether or not you need rest or activity or inspiration? Ask yourself what you need right now and move yourself into a position where you can get it. Are you trying to snatch 20 minutes' rest in your office? Move into the living room for that 20 minutes and relax completely, away from your work. Are you reading this while sitting on a stool in the kitchen, when there is somewhere else nearby where you would feel more inspired? By thinking over these questions, you are practicing Feng Shui at a very basic, immediate level.

APPROPRIATE PLACEMENT   Take some time to consider where you could move that would make reading this book a more supportive, inspiring experience. For example, you might want to sit in an armchair in a relaxing environment. Maybe you need to soak in a hot bath or sit outside in the fresh air. Maybe the location you are reading in is entirely wrong and you need to move to a city café or a beautiful field?

CHANGING NEEDS   Work out what you really want to be doing at this moment and also what you need to be doing. If you are reading this in bed while feeling really tired, the chances are that you are about to drop off, so you will neither absorb what the book says nor enjoy high quality sleep! Put the book down, turn the light off, and settle down comfortably to doze off, while promising yourself to put some time aside tomorrow to read when you are more alert.

Your responsibility for your health starts with making sure that wherever you are situated at any one time is appropriate to your current needs—bearing in mind that those are constantly changing. So always move yourself into a position that can really support you in what you are trying to do at any given time.

Often we need to share things that we read with others in order to draw further inspiration from them.

Listen to your body. A busy mind can sometimes drown out your instinctual knowledge of what is healthy for you.

right here, right now

To attain good health, you must learn to ascertain what you need right now, in the present—as opposed to what you usually need, or what you needed yesterday. You may think you should have a calming cup of herbal tea while sitting in the garden enjoying the sun, but what you may actually need is an energizing cup of coffee in a busy café. Try not to make presumptions about your body without considering how you really feel.

KNOW YOURSELF Throw away your preconceptions and work out exactly what you need at any one time. Also, avoid pressure from other people who think they know what you need; however well-meaning they are, they may not necessarily know what is right for you. Taking your power back involves courage, albeit on a very small basis at first. Even simple decisions, such as which

seat to choose in a restaurant or on the subway, where to buy your newspaper, or which checkout to use at your local supermarket, will make you feel better, healthier, and more energetic, grounded, and supported when you make the right choice, giving you a greater feeling of overall well-being.

Make your choices carefully, because they reflect your personality.

Create your living space with care by listening to your intuition. Make changes that reflect your aspirations and benefit your health.

Choose fabrics with care — they create the internal landscape of your house.

BE CREATIVE From that small starting point, you will gain confidence to design your living space along similar lines, without having to follow anyone else's rules. To begin with, tackle just one room. You need to work out which room is most important to your health. If you need rest and recuperation, concentrate on your bedroom or bathroom. If you need inspiration, stimulation, and vitality, look at one of the reception rooms, the living room, or the study. If you need deep, nurturing care, tackle the kitchen. Before you start, remember that when you are healthy you have no excuse for not achieving and being happy, because being ill can be an excuse for dodging life's challenges. Have the courage to be healthy!

the healthy bathroom

So many of us today feel that we never get enough rest and relaxation. If this is the case in your life, there are two areas to look at: the bathroom and the bedroom. Look for signs of imbalance in your bathroom, and you may solve your problem.

Solitude can provide as many opportunities for fun as outings with our friends.

Adrenaline junkies often multitask— reading in the bath, for example, can eclipse an opportunity for deep relaxation.

ADRENALINE JUNKIES We all know people who believe that stress equals fun. They rush around, living on black coffee and too little sleep, thinking that if they're not on the run, they can't be enjoying themselves. They may fear loneliness, so by keeping busy they exclude solitary periods from their lives. The ability to relax is about winter and water energy, so when a house's occupants can't relax, problems often appear in the bathroom.

SIGNS AND SYMPTOMS In the home of an adrenaline junkie, the design and decor of the bathroom will probably not be well thought out; the structure is likely to

Creating a clear, ordered bathroom containing just the necessary toiletries will make the space an oasis of calm.

have been "inherited" from previous occupants. It will look untidy, with damp towels left on the floor and toiletries spilling across shelves. The medicine cupboard may be crammed full, and there will be a few half-empty bottles of shampoo on the end of the bath. There may also be problems with leaks or dripping taps, which need fixing.

Cultivate a more selective approach to your toiletries to avoid unnecessary clutter.

SELF-HELP Clear the room out and throw away items that are likely to remain unused. In future, just buy one high-quality product that you really like, rather than several bargains. In general, take life at a more considered pace. Go out to two enjoyable social engagements a week, rather than 16 so-so events. Remember that enjoying your life has to do with quality, not quantity.

the healthy bedroom

If you're on the go all day long, racing from one engagement to another, by the time you fall into bed, you're probably overtired, stressed-out, and suffering from caffeine-generated jitters. After a restless night's sleep, you tumble out of bed feeling worn out and deprived of good quality rest, and then start again.

BREAK THE CYCLE You can break the vicious cycle by making your bedroom a more restful place in which to sleep. For a start, reduce the number of mirrors in your bedroom, or work toward a position where there are no mirrors in the room at all. Specifically, avoid mirrors or mirrored wardrobes facing the bed. Mirrors speed up chi, and this is the last thing you need in a bedroom. If you really cannot bear to exclude mirrors from your bedroom altogether, either hang one inside the wardrobe door, where you will only see it when the door is open, or if it is on an open wall, drape a large piece of silk or a scarf over it before you get into your bed at night.

If you wake up feeling tired and drained each day, you will not be able to live or work to your full potential.

CREATE CALM Make sure that your bedroom is totally dedicated to sleep and relaxation. Move out any objects like computers, because they will remind you of work, and televisions, since these are too stimulating. Also remove anything that involves aerobic exertion, like rowing machines or an exercise bike.

CAREFULLY PLACE THE BED Take a walk around your bedroom, decide which would be the place you would most like to sleep in, and see if it is practical for you to move your bed to that spot. Forget what other people say about the best place for your bed, and work out which spot feels the safest and most secure to you.

If your bedroom is a south-facing room, make sure that you can cover the windows easily, during the day as well as at night, so that you can keep it dark when you want to sleep, and avoid really bright abrasive colors. Keep red, orange, and even yellow shades to a minimum, and move toward using softer purple, lilac, blue, pink, and peach colors in the decor. Place a very soft and absorbent carpet or a few rugs on the floor. This will also slow chi down and enable you to get a good night's sleep.

Rugs will slow the flow of chi and make your bedroom more restful.

Calming colors, soft floor coverings, and heavy curtains are important features for a relaxing bedroom.

Decorate with soft pastel shades

Make sure your curtains block out the light

Keep bright shades to a minimum

Lay soft carpet

the healthy
reception room 1

In contrast to those people who constantly wear themselves out by taking on too much, many of us feel that we just don't have the stamina to cope with the activities that confront us every day—no matter how much sleep we get every night.

STUCK IN A RUT? Perhaps your problem is not that you have too much energy, but the reverse. Do you often feel sleepy and lethargic, heavy-headed, dull, or thoroughly bored? Do you doze off as soon as you sit down in an armchair to watch television or pick up a book? These symptoms are often exhibited by people who have got "stuck" in their lives and who are feeling uninspired. They are often enclosed in some kind of hemmed-in position—perhaps because it started off feeling cozy and safe, but has now turned into a trap that prevents them from growing and developing further. To increase your energy levels, you should tackle one of your reception rooms—perhaps your living room or your study. Choose a room in which you spend a considerable length of time every day.

Dozing off in front of the television is a sure sign of stagnant energy. Use Feng Shui in your living room to remedy the situation.

CLEAN THE INSIDE The first thing to do is to look at the windows. Clear any clutter off the window-sill and reduce layers of window covers. If you have blinds and drapes, consider looping the curtains back and pulling the

blinds right up, or even taking one away for a while. If you have muslin at the window, pull it out of the way or remove it altogether for a while. Give the windows a thorough cleaning, then take time to carry out a thorough space-clearing ritual (see Family Harmony) throughout the room to get rid of staleness and to energize chi, which will in turn have an invigorating effect on you.

To encourage good communication, arrange seating around the coffee table rather than the television.

CLEAR THE OUTSIDE Clean the outside of the windows and cut back any plants obscuring them. Look at ways to increase their capacity for giving you more light and energy. This would extend to objects outside the house that obscure the view, like a large tree or tall fence. Instead of coming from the angle of "Shall I cut that tree down?", ask yourself how you would feel if the tree was no longer there; this will give you more accurate information.

127

the healthy
reception room 2

Once you have cleared your windows and the space within your chosen room, look around it and remove anything that you feel is no longer nurturing to you. Work out which items in the room inspire and stimulate you, and which items bore and stupefy you.

THE TELEVISION If the room is a living room, very often the television set will be in a key position. It may be the first thing you see as you enter the room, and the good-quality seating will probably be arranged around it. Consider moving the set to a more low-key spot. Television takes away a lot of our vitality and most of the time doesn't inspire us, because we often end up watching programs that are not challenging.

Low lighting can illuminate the dark corners of a room and remedy areas of stagnant space.

SEATING AND LIGHTING If your living room is full of cozy, squashy furniture, you may have made it too much like a bedroom. If that is the case, you could consider moving or giving away some of the soft furnishings, and increasing the energy level by changing the lighting. Boost the low-level ambient lighting, so that there is not one single source of light, but several around the room. Install a couple of task-lights, which will ensure that the place in which you plan to play the piano, read a book, or write a novel is well lit. You might consider hanging a curving mirror on the wall to speed up the flow of chi.

WORKROOMS If it's your study that needs attention, look at how you've organized your belongings around you within the room. Are they accessible? Or do you have to wade through loads of abandoned projects, representing failure, in order to get to the ones you want to begin? Maybe you never do get around to embarking on new projects, because you're surrounded by outdated old ones. Make sure that you clear them off your desk to enable you to start fresh.

If you've decided to redecorate your study, do it with shiny, rather than matte, surfaces and think in terms of polished wood, rather than the dull, distressed finish. Don't introduce too many sharp abrasive angles, however, because these will make you feel stressed.

Try to keep your study tidy and free of distractions. Natural light will help you to concentrate.

the healthy kitchen 1

In the practice of Feng Shui, the kitchen has always been a very important room in the house since ancient times. The way in which you treat your kitchen is a good indication of the way in which you treat yourself.

KITCHEN CHAOS If you believe you've never really enjoyed the best of health and don't feel that you've been well looked after or have looked after yourself, you should concentrate your remedies in your kitchen. Take a look at it. Does it look neglected and uncared for? Is there a "just-passing-through" feel to the room? Is it a place you only dash into to reheat packaged food?

SIGNS AND SYMPTOMS Perhaps you suffer from a great deal of anxiety over your eating habits. You may feel that you eat far too much of the "wrong" food (which you like) and not enough of the "right" food (which you don't like). This can often lead to a situation in which you no longer see eating as a pleasurable experience, but as full of tension and stress. Maybe you are constantly on a diet—or perhaps you eat a lot of junk food, which is another way of looking for comfort?

What does the arrangement of your kitchen say about your lifestyle and general eating habits?

TAKE A SEAT Go into your kitchen and sit down. You may find there isn't even a place where you can! If you can't find a seat, organize one. Even if your seat is a simple barstool, paint it in a color that you like, so that you derive more enjoyment from it.

LET GO OF THE PAST Look around the room and list everything that reminds you that you haven't lived up to your expectation of yourself. Then, despite the expense, get rid of these items. They are a constant sign that you've failed to achieve, and that you haven't sat and listened to what you yourself would like and made allowances for your personal circumstances. Objects that reflect this could be food processors, which always take so long to clean that you are reluctant to use them, or that big casserole dish for a hearty meal for six—face up to the fact that you're never going to use it!

Whether your kitchen is a cozy room with a wood-burning oven or a more modern design, it is the heart of the house, and needs attention.

EMPTY YOUR CUPBOARDS Go through your food cupboard and throw away anything past its use-by date or that looks like the kind of thing you wouldn't want to eat if you saw it in a friend's home. It's merely taking up space and making you feel bad—you are never going to eat it.

131

the healthy kitchen 2

It's very important to set up your kitchen in a way that it nurtures you—but don't arrange it with unrealistic expectations in mind, since this will only result in frustration and stress. Make changes that are practical and supportive in terms of the way you live, rather than to suit the way that other people expect you to live.

CELEBRATE YOUR FREEDOM   Once you've discarded the signs of failure, start thinking about the things that would make you feel really cheerful and then set your kitchen up in a way that will make you happy. Allow yourself to spend six months eating chocolate cake, if that's what you want to do. But before you start, buy a book with a good recipe for chocolate cake in it, some nice plates, and a colorful cake tin, so that you make the whole process a celebration.

Replace unwanted presents and hand-me-downs with dishes that suit your taste.

TAKE IT EVEN FURTHER   Then just pause beyond the idea of the chocolate cake and ask yourself what living on chocolate cake would make you feel, and if there is anything else that would make you feel that way. Along with the objects for chocolate cake, you might buy containers to store wholesome bread or a dishwasher so that you might take time to make homemade soup without worrying about doing the dishes. It's all about creating a realistic environment. In the same way that exercise regimes fail if you set unrealistic goals, space will not work for you if it is not organized in a realistic way.

SET ACHIEVABLE GOALS If you don't have time to cook, rather than reheat fast food, make a healthy fresh chicken salad sandwich—it won't take much longer. If the only fresh food you are going to eat all week will be, for example, tomatoes, buy high-quality, organic tomatoes rather than spending money on groceries that you'll throw away. Don't make unrealistic demands on yourself in terms of how you expect to look after yourself.

If you have any money to spend, equip yourself to achieve what is achievable within the constraints of your lifestyle. Don't buy an expensive oven if you never have time to cook; buy a nice sandwich toaster or a juicer instead. I visit so many houses with beautifully equipped kitchens—yet their families live on take-outs! They would be better off investing in a really attractive garbage can, because that is where all the discarded food wrapping ends up! Take time to make yourself a priority.

An excess of kitchen equipment can make you feel pressured to become a supercook and instill a sense of continual failure.

using color for health

Many people never seem to enjoy consistent good health, constantly suffering from annoying, chronic complaints, like asthma, eczema, rhinitis, and hayfever. All of these illnesses result from a depressed immune system, and a good way to deal with them is by tackling the overall color scheme of your living space.

An excess of white in your surroundings could leave you open to minor complaints by depressing your energy levels.

SIGNS AND SYMPTOMS Sufferers are often metal element people astrologically. According to Chinese philosophy, the metal element vibrates at the same level as the color white, and when I am consulted by people who are suffering from a number of minor complaints, I would expect to see an awful lot of white around their house, or at least walls that are painted white with an apricot, peach, or blue tint.

LOOK FOR CLUES If you recognize your house in this description, look around and identify where there are splashes of color in the form of clothes, cosmetics, and even food. While most of the areas of your life are colored in pastels, there may be one part which is sporting vivid colors, and creating a huge

imbalance. Rectify this by initially deciding what color you can use to balance the situation. This can be a difficult question to answer, so start by picking the colors you like. What colors do you like to wear? What color foods do you like to eat? What colors would you like to have around you when you're on vacation? What colors make you feel happy or relaxed?

One of the easiest ways to introduce color into your home is in the food that you choose—try a new color every week!

INTRODUCE COLOR You might come up with a range of colors, such as blues or reds. Think about introducing them into your living space. You don't have to totally redecorate; just buy items such as some new dishes or a flower vase or pillow in your favorite colors. When you're shopping, think about buying food in the same colors; for example, if you like warm, rich reds, raid the fruit section in the supermarket for raspberries and strawberries, and buy tomatoes, red peppers, beets, and kidney beans. Hopefully, introducing a broader range of colors into your life will help to improve your general health.

CASE STUDY

I did one consultation for a man who was highly asthmatic and his whole house was decorated white, apart from a splash of navy blue in the form of his suits hung on an open rack system (the rest of his clothes were white too!). The only piece of color he would allow me to introduce was a bowl of fruit—and that had to be a white bowl with only one type of fruit in it, at that! Once you've got "hooked" on the color white, it can be very hard to let go!

letting go

People who live in minimalist surroundings are often those who have metal energy and a tendency to try to control every aspect of their lives. When they learn that it's okay to let go sometimes, they find that their lives become a lot easier and happier.

Minimalist decor can make you feel as if you're living your life in a restrained way— in black and white rather than in color.

THE NEED FOR CONTROL The lives of metal energy people tend to improve as they get older. They often grow up in an unsupportive environment, which gradually wears down their immune system as a child, because they don't get sufficient grounding. They have a tendency to thrive in later years, but are often too depleted to bring about this flowering. Because they are unfulfilled, they try to express themselves by controlling their environment, so you often find that people who suffer from minor immune deficiency ailments are excessively tidy. They tend to be dependent on minimalist surroundings, devoid of stimulation.

CASE STUDY

If you are a bit of a "control freak," try breaking up the atmosphere by introducing a humorous element into your living space. One client of mine who was very organized and controlling worked in real estate. I carried out a consultation in his office and as a result, suggested that he introduce some humor into it. He brought in a toy airplane which flew around on a spring, a wall plaque with a smiling rising sun, and one of his son's toys. The next time I visited the office, these items had really altered the atmosphere and loosened it up.

INTRODUCE SOME CHAOS If your environment is very ordered and there is a definite place for everything, to the point where it is taken to extremes, introduce a little bit of chaos into your living space. Choose five things you really like—a book, a jacket, a scarf, a plant, and a bowl of fruit, for example—and move them out of their usual places. Leave the book on a coffee table, drape the jacket over the back of a chair, hang the scarf across the window, and so on. Make sure that the number of objects you use is odd so as to introduce movement, because even numbers are very static. Make an effort to introduce an element of play into your environment instead of trying always to keep it rigidly under control, because that controlling aspect of your personality will stress your immune system eventually causing you ill health.

A few objects placed in a haphazard way can provoke a little movement in an otherwise static life.

the celestial animals 1

In assessing the Feng Shui of a house, the Ancient Chinese practitioners would traditionally consider the landscape that surrounded the building in terms of the four Celestial Animals: the Tortoise, the Tiger, the Dragon, and the Phoenix.

OUR INHERITANCE Health isn't something that begins and ends with our bodies. There are influences way beyond us in the here and now that still affect us and stretch into our past and future; these include our genetic inheritance, our upbringing, and both our immediate environment and our far-reaching environment.

OUR HORIZONS We have to check whether the space we are in right now is supporting us. During our upbringing, have we been given the notion that we have a future in front of us? Have we been given the idea that it's safe to move into a position where we can fulfill ourselves? Have we been given shining long-distance horizons? Do we have people in our life that have gone before us, who are potential role models? Are we living in a society that allows us to expect to find fulfillment?

In metaphysical terms, the landscape that surrounds you is made up of your past, your present, and your potential future.

THE TORTOISE To take that concept from the human experience and put it into Feng Shui terms, we can look at it as a landscape that surrounds us. With regard to history and support from the past, our living space needs to have strong support to the rear. If you look behind your house, you would hope to see symbols of a strong, solid past, with deep roots, ancestry, and protection. In a rural environment, this could be a distant hill, an ancient tree, or an old brick wall. In an urban environment, it might be an attractive building that's older than your house, or a symbol of your heritage, like a church. The Chinese call this the "Tortoise," and it plays a role like the back of a chair, to support you from behind. If you don't have this kind of structure behind your house, you can substitute an object representing longevity and deep roots, like a standing stone or a trellis of climbing plants, anchored further by a stone bench stationed in front of it.

The Tortoise, Yuan Wu, represents nurture and stablility.

A trellis and stone bench in your backyard can represent support.

139

the celestial animals 2

Think of the building in which you live as a person, requiring elbow room, but at the same time needing to have someone within reach for support. There should be support on both sides of your home to represent the support you receive in your current life, but you also need freedom to move and expand.

Wu, the tiger, and Wen, the dragon, represent vitality, poise, and balance.

The row of houses below introduces imbalance to the central house, and does not allow its occupants the possibility of growth.

TIGER, DRAGON, AND PHOENIX In an urban situation, hopefully, your house will not be wedged between two bigger buildings, because this will not give you space to grow, or between two buildings where one is much larger than the other, since this would create imbalance. On either side of your living space you should be looking for symbols that represent vitality, life, poise, and balance. (In Chinese terms, these are called the "Tiger" and the "Dragon.") So if you were in a row of houses, you would want to be situated between two

The central house is overshadowed by its more substantial neighbors

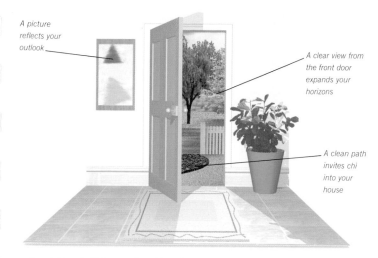

A picture reflects your outlook

A clear view from the front door expands your horizons

A clean path invites chi into your house

flourishing buildings rather than between a structure that is very run-down and a house that the occupants can't sell. In a rural environment, your house needs to be in balance with the landscape features around it.

What you will also need is bright chi ahead—in other words good times coming up. When you stand at your front door and look out, you should see something bright and inspirational (in Chinese terms, the "Phoenix").

Whether you open your front door to a view of natural scenery or a busy urban road, keep your threshold clean and inviting.

A GOOD OUTLOOK In an urban environment, it would be very propitious to look out onto a park and to have some space between your front door and the next object, whether it's a fence, wall, or road. If you have it, keep that space clean and swept, and put beautiful things in it. Even if you're in a narrow street and your front door opens straight onto the sidewalk, make sure you sweep the sidewalk and put beautiful objects on either side of the front door. In a rural environment, you would hope for a clear view of the countryside, so that your horizons, both physical and metaphysical, appear boundless.

Feng Huang, the phoenix, represents bright inspiration and good fortune.

health hazards

When you are moving into a new home or working space, it is as important to consider the features of the landscape that surrounds it as it is to pay attention to the structure of the building itself. Both will have an important impact on your life.

Vibration of the grounds of a house from passing trains can have a de-stabilizing influence on its occupants.

UNHEALTHY ENVIRONMENTS Another factor that will contribute to your overall health is what surrounds your house, which is the physical outside-world equivalent to who your friends are. You can't get well and healthy if you are mixing with friends who constantly run you down, advise you to do things that are hazardous to you, and deplete your energy. In the same way, it's hard to be healthy if your ability to enjoy health is compromised by things like power lines, disturbances in the ground close to where your home is built (subway systems), or very busy roads.

SIGNS AND SYMPTOMS Before you buy a home, look out for clues that indicate a degenerating environment, like dead trees or subsidence, since these can indicate an unhealthy situation. The close proximity of looming, angular buildings with sharp edges that cut chi pointing toward your living space is also not advisable. Buildings with this kind of attribute are only good to live in for a very short time and can be used to get you out of a "stuck" position, but you should see

them only as short-term living spaces. Living in close proximity to cemeteries, and institutions inhabited by large groups of people who are unhealthy or unhappy, is also inadvisable.

If you wish to carry out a domestic conversion of an old building, consider its past life carefully.

Furthermore, you should always be wary of living in a space that was not originally intended as a dwelling place, but was converted from, for instance, an old church or hospital. This could have implications for your health.

CASE STUDY

I was once called to an employment agency in Central London where they'd suffered from continual staffing problems, and when I walked to the window, I saw a black, shiny building with the angle of its walls pointing straight through toward their windows. We moved the desks of the key workers so that they were out of the line of the cutting chi. Because the cutting chi was setting up abrasive energy, there were a lot of spiky images within the office, so I suggested they try to get the chi to settle down by introducing calmer artwork. The office subsequently experienced some more staffing changes, which is quite normal after a Feng Shui consultation, but things were really beginning to settle down the last time I spoke to them.

QUICK FIXES

1. Clear out any stagnant water in nearby ponds, maintain drains, and mend guttering.

2. The kitchen is very often the key to poor health, so start your Feng Shui remedies there.

3. Relieve stress by clearing out your bathroom.

4. If you're feeling a lot of stress, look at how much dark red you've got around the house and get rid of some of it.

5. If you're not sleeping well, remove all of the mirrors from your bedroom.

CAREER AND
WORKPLACE

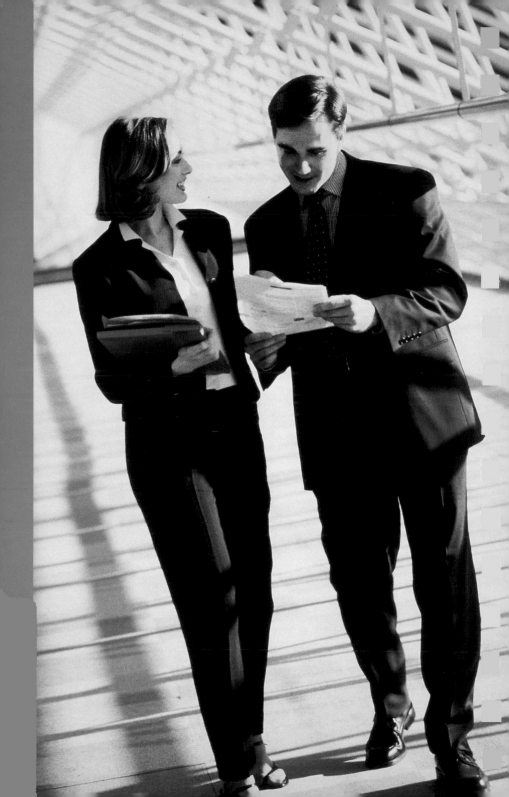

career and workplace

If you feel stuck in a rut at work or feel the need for a total change of career, Feng Shui can help you to change your situation. It is possible to introduce Feng Shui practices into the workplace to help you to either move on or to perform more effectively in your current job. And the joy of it is, it's so subtle, your colleagues probably won't even notice.

living to work or working to live?

Our work is the way that we recreate ourselves on a basic level. The money we earn pays for our food and shelter, so if we're not happy in our work, we feed this back through our whole life system. It's impossible to pretend that while we're unhappy at work, it is compensated for by a great home life.

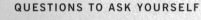

QUESTIONS TO ASK YOURSELF

1. How do you define work?

2. Do you think of work as something you have to endure so that you can earn money and enjoy the rest of your life?

3. Is your work a tool to negotiate your own growth and development?

4. Are you hiding behind work? Do you allow your employer to impose on you, or do you impose on yourself, so that you have little free time?

5. Are you proud of what you do to earn a living?

Work can be an important means of self-expression.

THE RIGHT JOB Many people express themselves through their work; it's a place where they can grow and develop, contribute their talent, and have it recognized by others. If you are feeling unhappy at work, perhaps it's because the job doesn't give you sufficient outlet to express yourself or because you don't receive recognition for your efforts when you do.

BLAMING OTHERS Maybe you blame your boss for your lack of fulfillment at work. If you do, however, you are giving someone else responsibility for what you do, which of course has the payoff that you can then blame that person for everything that goes wrong in your life. However, nine times out of ten, it is not someone else who is limiting you, but you who are limiting yourself.

If you imagine that a stressful working life earns you a fulfilling retirement, you are shutting your eyes to the present moment.

CHANGE YOUR ATTITUDE Perhaps you've been taught that work has to be miserable, boring drudgery in order to justify earning money from it. Many people believe that they have to do something they don't enjoy to justify the money they earn in return and that if they have a miserable working life, they will have fun in their retirement— but it may be too late then! Liberate yourself with the notion that it is possible to get paid for doing something that you do really well and that you love doing.

True fulfillment may mean changing career paths completely.

wood energy

In trying to create new opportunities in your career, what you are attempting to do in your life is to create the possibility of springtime, which is, of course, related to wood energy. It's like raking piles of dead leaves away, so you can see signs of fresh shoots and new life.

The Chinese symbol for Wood, an element characterized by rising life-energy.

WOOD ENERGY This type of energy is characterized by upward movement, so to encourage it, move things away from ground level. Think of the movement that occurs in nature in the spring—sap rising—and try to encourage it throughout your life. If you have a pile of books on the floor, move them up onto a shelf. If you habitually throw your bag on the floor when you come into your living space, start to hang it on a hook.

GOOD PLACEMENT Place things where they will take the eye upward, so, if you have a vase of flowers, instead of placing it on a low coffee table, think about raising it to a higher shelf or window sill. If you buy a new picture, hang it just fractionally higher than you would usually.

APPROPRIATE COLORS In your color scheme, you could consider introducing little touches of green. Don't decorate an entire room in the color—a winter landscape doesn't turn into summer overnight, but arrives gradually, with splashes of green increasing as the spring progresses, so introduce hints of green in the form of pictures, mirror frames, or blinds.

PLANTS Be careful about using plants to introduce wood energy. If you put a large plant in a small space, check that it doesn't dominate the space and stop chi flowing naturally. Plants can do good work in generating wood energy, but be prepared to put them outside if you feel they start to take over a room and wood energy is becoming excessive.

PERSONALITY TRAITS People with an imbalance in energy may start to become too forward-thinking and sometimes don't stand firmly on their feet in the present, because they're looking too much into the future. If you start to get irritable and angry, you keep raising your voice, or you become prone to headaches, the chances are that you're introducing too much wood energy, so take some time out to appreciate what you've got in the present.

Wood energy can be cultivated by introducing some simple wooden ornaments.

Lead the energy upward with ornaments placed high up

Use large plants in moderation, as they speed up chi

High, upright seating encourages wood energy

are you ready to change?

If you are not feeling fulfilled and recognized through your work, ask yourself what can you do to change it and when would you like it to change? To answer those questions, you need to think about your own attitude toward change.

RESISTANCE People have a huge resistance to change and tend to feed back into their ideas of themselves. Even if you do blame your boss for not recognizing your talent and allowing you to move on in terms of promotion, there is usually some kind of payoff in accepting that particular situation. For example, if the work you do is not too demanding, it doesn't set any challenges that you can't meet. If the job you are currently occupying is a compromise for you because you can't get the job of your dreams, the payoff may be that if you were offered that ideal post, you would have to work much harder to achieve meaningful results.

SIGNS AND SYMPTOMS Once you've considered why you are in your current dissatisfied position at work and have worked out your reasons for staying in it, look at how you might cope with both the good and bad things that would be the result of moving out of it. How well you cope with change can often be demonstrated by the way you make use of your immediate environment. People who don't cope with change very well are inclined to physically hem themselves in in the way they set out the furniture in their living space. They also tend to surround

If you truly want to be recognized for the work that you do, you will instinctively create changes to make it happen.

themselves with objects that keep them firmly pinned down in the past, so they're not very aware and conscious of what's going on around them in the present.

AT HOME   How much clutter do you surround yourself with in your home? How many items do you have around you that don't represent the person that you want to be or the career that you want to move into? How many objects in your immediate environment reflect what you achieved in the past or the compromises and duties that you've reluctantly felt forced to take on?

Be aware of what the objects that surround you are saying about your ability to cope with the future.

AT WORK   The same questions can be applied to your work surroundings. Look around your desk and see how many incomplete tasks and projects are lying on it. These tasks represent the dead wood that must be cut out of your environment if you are going to change your life.

A cluttered workspace indicates a failure to move forward.

clutter-clearing your office

If you often experience a feeling of dread when you confront your desk each morning, clear away everything but the absolute essentials. Not only will this help to improve your working life, but your boss should be impressed by the air of efficiency around your desk!

THE THREE-BOX SYSTEM A good way to start this is to take three boxes. In one of them, put the things that you definitely want to keep; in another, put items that you know you've outgrown and can safely discard. In the third, put the objects that you feel ambivalent about, either because you think you ought to keep them, as they were given to you by people you like and respect, or because you have a sentimental attachment to them, even though you know you've moved on from them. Start to examine the emotions that the latter arouse in you, and this will gradually lead you to a point where you feel able to let them go.

The three-box system helps you to prioritize your work papers and personal belongings with a view to clearing out and moving on.

CLEAR OUT COMPUTER FILES Obviously, visible clutter in terms of old files and outdated case studies is easy to deal with, but don't forget the less visible stuff. Clear out the clogged-up memory of your computer and clean off any disks that now contain redundant information.

CASE STUDY

I did one consultation at a health practice, where every staff member was constantly overloaded with work and stressed out. I found out that they were holding on to medical records far beyond the legal requirements, so they were effectively storing the energetic imprints of thousands of sick people in their work space. To prevent themselves from being pinned down by the weight of this overwhelming cloud of inherited energy, the practice needed to clear out all of the unnecessary files. Every item, from a key to a pen, holds a certain quality of chi and carries an energetic memory of all the things it's done and all the places it's been to. If we look around our space at all the energetic memories, we can see why we might be held back.

IMAGINE THE FUTURE Even if you're not certain which direction you want your career, or life, to follow, when you start to clutter-clear, you will begin to dismantle your old concept of work by clearing away things that are no longer valid. And as the work continues, you will find that a picture of what you would like to do instead, or the person you would like to be in future, will start to emerge.

A clear desk invites clarity of thought and encourages efficiency.

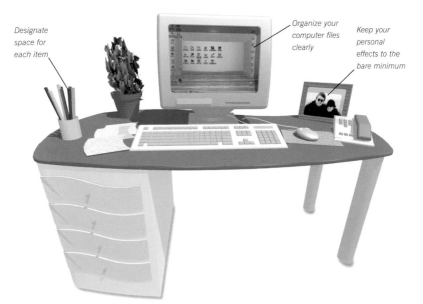

Designate space for each item

Organize your computer files clearly

Keep your personal effects to the bare minimum

moving on

The objects that surround us help to define who we are. If you are looking for a promotion or a change of job or even career, bear in mind that you should keep objects around you that reflect the position you are working toward.

OLD ENERGY If objects don't serve to nurture and inspire you anymore, they're not going to help you to move on. Think about whether you still want to display photographs and certificates of past achievements on your office wall; they identify who you were rather than who you are now.

NEW POSSIBILITIES Your office may be lined with shelves full of reference books. If you bought them in the hope of winning a promotion but didn't succeed, they will represent failure to you. Alternatively, if they are college books, they represent past successes and keep you firmly fixed in your past idea of who you are and what you have already achieved, rather than who you are now and what you can go on to achieve. By throwing or giving those books away, you won't be giving away your achievements—you will carry those with you always—but you are opening the door to new opportunities for success. If we let go of past success and failure, we create space for new possibilities.

Graduation is a doorway to the future, not a tie to the past. Move through the doorway and close it behind you.

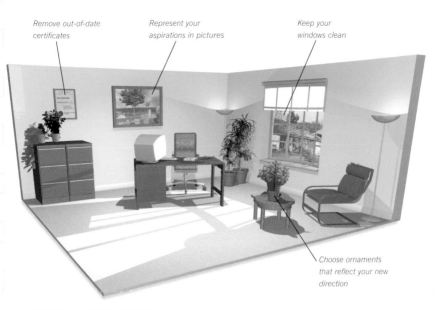

Remove out-of-date
certificates

Represent your
aspirations in pictures

Keep your
windows clean

Choose ornaments
that reflect your new
direction

MAKE A STATEMENT If you are looking for a total change of career, surround yourself with objects that make a statement about where you're going. For example, you may be an accountant who hopes to become a freelance garden designer. Clutter-clear the reminders of the old job, such as professional certificates and accounting textbooks, and bring in new images relating to your aspirations— pictures of gardens or beautiful plants. Any images you have around you should help you to build on the direction that you want to be following.

USE THE PHOENIX To assist you in achieving your ambitions, make sure that wherever you sit to work you are stimulated by what lies before you. That doesn't necessarily mean you have to face a window. If you have no option but to face a wall, put a picture of a landscape or a bird in flight up in front of you rather than facing a blank wall or inappropriate picture or shelves full of junk.

Move on in your working life by making your surroundings reflect the future.

increasing your ability to move on

It's one thing to dream of recreating yourself—you may be able to create a very clear image of how you would like to be spending your time—but now you need to achieve that ambition and make it real. To do this, you will need to bring your ambition from the realm of ideas—the etheric realm—into the real manifest world.

FORWARD MOVEMENT I've already started to talk about bringing things into your space that symbolize the way in which you'd prefer to spend your time and the person that you'd like to be. We now have to look at making alterations to the quality of chi in your environment to help to manifest these plans. Basically, you must begin to create an environment where forward movement and directed action are possible.

Clean your windows to illuminate your home and allow a free passage of energy. Dispel redundent energy by throwing out breakages.

PRACTICAL TIPS First, you could make some physical changes to your environment to increase your ability to move on. Clean your windows, both inside and out, and make sure that you don't have lots of broken objects or incomplete tasks lying around your home. Tie up all the loose ends in your physical space and also in your emotional and mental space. You might realize that it's time to let go of certain friendships and to start frequenting different places and moving in different circles. Make some space for new

opportunities to come into your life by bringing any kind of mental or emotional situation that has been dragging on for a while to a conclusion. Actively let go of your past.

New friendships bring new experiences and help you to let go of old ways of thinking.

FOLLOW THROUGH   As well as doing a thorough clutter-clear of your work environment, you need to follow through to the rest of your home in a steady, well-managed way. There is a recognized order to this work. Start at the hallway first, around the area of your front door initially, outside and inside. When you've completely clutter-cleared the hallway, look at each of the main living areas, such as the reception rooms and lounge. Once you've done those, work through the water energy areas—the still, resting areas, such as the bedroom or any room where you sit to meditate—to clarify and calm the energy. Finally, clean out the kitchen and bathroom.

Areas of stillness in your house will need to be cleared of any stagnant energy.

directing chi

It is not enough to simply clear the clutter out of your home—this is only the first step in Feng Shui. What you need to do next is to work with the chi in and around your house. You need to be aware of the flow of chi so that it flows through your home in a way that will bring you optimum benefits.

SHAPE THE FLOW When you've finished that thorough clutter-clear in your home, you can then begin to shape the energy within your house in a similarly organized way. To do this you could first look at the routes through your home. Starting at the front gate, observe the route you customarily take through your home. Check that all of its pathways, steps, and stairways are completely clear, and make sure that any railings at the side of any stairs to the front door are firmly fixed and safe. If you have a front porch, give it some attention and open it up by clearing out any clutter.

Connect all the passageways in your house in a continuous flow. The front path is as much a part of your home as the hall.

DIRECT THE FLOW When you have done that, the next thing to look at is the hall. Obviously, you've already clutter-cleared it, so you should now try to make the chi more directed, by, for example, putting a runner or a rug down on the floor to speed it up. However, if you feel that the chi is rushing through your hallway too quickly already, put down an oval rug to slow things down. Continue the process by slowly working your way through the whole house, being very aware of how the energy is moving. This process is all about linking one area to another smoothly, so make sure that all areas of connection, such as landings and passageways, are cleared.

THE LAST STEP When you've done everything else, it is finally time to pay some attention to your attic, which is a place that is all about movement in the future and spiritual growth. Make sure that you work through this entire process in the right order, because otherwise it will be difficult to clear out your attic until the other tasks are complete. However, if you've done everything else in the correct way, this should now prove to be quite easy. There is no need to rush this work. Do it at your own pace and in your own time, and while you're doing it, make sure that you're very aware of what's happening in your life and how it's changing as a result of the clearing you are doing. The final thing you should do is to express some gratitude to the universe for anything good that's now coming your way.

Simply looking at a pile of clutter can feel uncomfortable—you can almost sense how it confuses the flow of energy in your home.

limitations in the workplace

However constricted we may feel within our place of work, by using a little careful thought and ingenuity, there are always ways in which we can employ a few simple Feng Shui principles to broaden our horizons—both symbolically and in real life.

If your work area feels claustrophobic, take action to change the space. If colleagues do not support your changes, it may be time to move on.

THE ROLE OF PERCEPTION We often feel limited as to how much Feng Shui we are able to introduce into our workspace, but those limitations are frequently based on our own perceptions. For example, if you are squeezed into a corner of an office behind a door and you feel that there's no way you can improve your environment, you probably feel manipulated and powerless by your position and by the people around you, so the whole situation is claustrophobic, both physically and mentally.

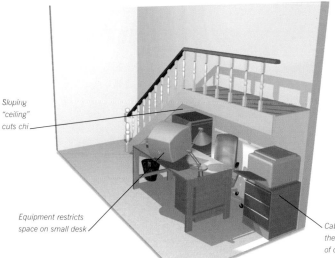

Sloping "ceiling" cuts chi

Equipment restricts space on small desk

Cabinet blocks the passage of chi

THE CALL TO ACTION   Maybe you had to be squeezed into that corner to encourage you to take action. You will need courage to make far-reaching changes—not in demanding more space or a new desk, but you could bring something of yourself into your work environment, which a lot of people feel is a very risky thing to do.

Personal items remind you of who you are and can help you to stay grounded.

AFFIRM YOUR IDENTITY   Bring from home or buy for yourself something that has to do with your sense of who you are. It could be a vase of flowers, a small picture, or an attractive cushion for your chair. If you take that small step, bigger steps become easier.

OBSERVE THE RESULTS   You may find that people around you instinctively respond with offers of support or a suggestion that you might like to move desks. On the other hand, people may appear to close in on you even more, which may make you rethink whether you should actually be in that job at all. The key is not to feel helpless but instead to make some changes to begin moving out of that position.

THE VICTIM MENTALITY   If you are very disempowered at work, there may be other areas of your life in which you've habitually become a victim. If you find yourself in a space upon which you cannot make any imprint at all, there is likely to be a bully somewhere who is creating that situation. To be bullied successfully, you have to allow it to happen. A simple change, which may seem very bold to you, will start to unravel the whole dynamic.

Small changes make a statement about you to others. By making a mark on your space at work, you reveal the person behind the job.

161

different layouts
for different jobs

There is no such thing as one single perfect workspace layout. Different layouts facilitate different jobs, whether you're a gardener, a teacher, or an accountant. We all need to establish a clear workspace that suits our particular needs.

Boundaries defining working space are important in outdoor environments as well as in office buildings.

WINDOW ACCESS If you have to be creative in your work, it may help to be able to look out at a view to take in creative energy. If you have to be focused to complete a task, however, it's better not to face a view, because you may find it too distracting.

DESK PLACEMENT If you are doing a job that requires a lot of planning or the initiating of projects, it's particularly important not to be stuck behind a desk facing a wall. You need to be facing a door or, failing that, a window, so that you can see a way out.

DIRECTIONAL TIPS If you are working on a task that you need to perform quickly, choose a south-facing room because this will help you to do something swiftly. When you want to plan and set up a project, work in an east-facing room and when you want to complete it, sit in a west-facing room. North-facing rooms are good for long-term projects, and north spaces can be very creative and inward-looking. Please note that in talking about the directions, I am referring to the way the windows, and not the doors (as is the Chinese way), are oriented. This is because window orientation is more important to the lives we live in the world of today.

Use north-facing rooms for long-term projects, east-facing rooms for planning, south-facing rooms for swift action, and west-facing rooms for project completion.

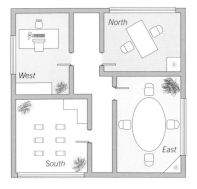

WHICH DIRECTION?

A west-facing room is beneficial for work in the health and fitness industry, management, or finance.

A south-facing room is beneficial for work in leisure and recreation, the travel industry, and the media.

An east-facing room is beneficial for work in marketing and projects that are in their planning stages.

A north-facing room is beneficial for work in the arts, research, and innovation.

taking up your position

In order to get the best out of yourself, whatever kind of job you're doing, it's important to understand the way chi flows through your working space. With this information you can position yourself in the right place in the room for whatever task you are carrying out.

DIRECTION OF ENERGY FLOW In the northern hemisphere, chi comes in through the door and flows clockwise around the room. In the southern hemisphere, chi moves round the room in a counterclockwise direction. However, there may be cases, in either hemisphere, where the flow of chi is reversed. Always follow your own instincts if you feel strongly that it is traveling in the reverse direction to that which you would normally expect.

OFFICES If you are about to start work on a project, it is best to sit at the beginning of the cycle, where the chi enters the room, so you will be able to initiate tasks that are full of inspiration. If you are trying to finish off a job, do it on the other side of the room, near the place where the chi exits, since this has to do with completion.

Be careful not to position desks and cabinets in places where they will block the flow of chi.

MEETING ROOMS If you are going into an important meeting, make sure that you arrive early so you can decide which will be the most effective part of the room for you to sit in. If others are arriving, don't get maneuvered into a bad position, because then people just won't hear you, no matter how good your ideas are. During the meeting, watch carefully how other people perform from different positions around the room, because then you can learn a lot about where to seat yourself at the next meeting in the same location.

As a general rule, in meetings, you should try to position yourself so that you are in the midst of a good, steady flow of chi. Don't allow yourself to get backed into a corner (where the chi may be stale) or stuck at the side of a looming piece of furniture. And always avoid sitting next to the door to the washroom; people will be constantly moving to and from that place, and as a consequence, the energy level there will be very low.

The low table at this meeting will allow everyone to be heard, while the chairs offer good support in an open space.

A curved table also allows an even balance of energy and will encourage everyone to contribute equally.

using chi to support you in meetings

Even if you are a party to business meetings that are not held within your own working area, there are ways in which you can manipulate the space available to ensure that you show your talent and abilities in their best light.

You can change your profile in meetings by choosing a seat that helps you to absorb or deflect the flow of chi.

TAKE CONTROL If you want to take the most powerful position in a meeting room, you should always try to sit diagonally opposite the door in most standard square offices. (However, do be aware of features that may alter the flow of chi, such as windows and large pieces of furniture.) In this position, you will work the hardest and be the highest profile person in the room.

TAKE A BACK SEAT If you are feeling uninspired and don't want it to be noticed, sit farther around the room, where the chi will pass on its way back out of the door. From here, you can pick up on other people's ideas and energy, and push it back out with your own slant.

ABSORB POWER If you walk into a room, watch where other people are sitting. If someone whom you find difficult or challenging is taking part, don't sit where you will absorb the downward energy from her, or you will assimilate a lot of her negative attitude. Position yourself on her other side, so that the chi passes through you first and you don't have to cope with her.

Take notice of the other energies involved in a meeting, and don't position yourself in the way of negative chi.

If you want somebody else to give you ideas and put a lot into a meeting, encourage him to sit in the most powerful position and sit on his immediate left, so he works hard at supplying you with ideas.

INTERVIEW TECHNIQUES If you are interviewing someone and you want to see what she's made of, place her in the most powerful position in the room and sit down the cycle from her. This will tell you what she is capable of. If you reverse this configuration, she'll learn a lot about you but you won't learn much about her. If you are the one being interviewed, choose the most powerful position in the room to show that you can take control. People instinctively know where these places are, even if they don't acknowledge it consciously, so the interviewer will be impressed by the way you handled the meeting.

taking all the help you can get

There is no need to approach any meeting with trepidation. When you walk into the place where the meeting is to be held, look around and note which features of the room will be helpful to you and which will be detrimental—and then seat yourself accordingly.

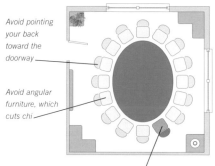

Avoid pointing your back toward the doorway

Avoid angular furniture, which cuts chi

Strong position

Listening position

Try to choose your seating position to suit whatever it is you want to achieve in the meeting.

THE BEST POSITION When you enter the room for a meeting, always be aware of where the windows are. Bearing in mind the importance of having Tortoise support, it's usually more important to get yourself in a position that gives you good support than to choose the best position in terms of the flow of chi. So if the most powerful position has a large window behind it or something obstructive like a large piece of furniture with an angle pointing into your back, choose the second or third best position.

CUTTING CHI You will often read in Feng Shui textbooks about the dangers of cutting chi, the angle where two planes join, whether they are walls or the sides of a piece of furniture. It is not as hazardous as many consultants claim, and can sometimes be used to your advantage, but the important thing is to ascertain where the angle is pointing. Try to let it hit you at the front of your body around the level of your heart. If one of these angles is pointing directly at the back of your neck or head, move immediately, because this will not be beneficial to you.

USE ANGLES In a brainstorming meeting, the angles of cutting chi may be beneficial since they accelerate fire energy, which is about illumination and activity. In this case, it would be good to align yourself with an angle, but only if you feel confident and sure of your position. Otherwise you will be thrown off balance and your energy will be scattered. You could also find that you're working really well for the first 15 minutes and then become very uncomfortable. In this position, too, you could be found out for not being the person that people hoped you were.

If you have something important to say but the power position has already been taken, great confidence is required to make use of cutting chi.

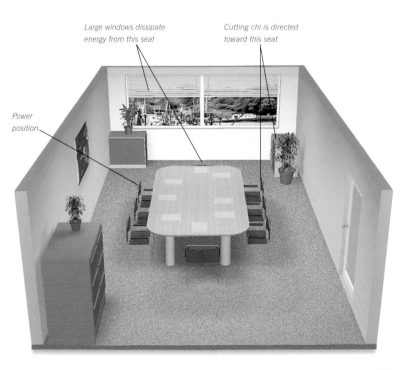

Large windows dissipate energy from this seat

Cutting chi is directed toward this seat

Power position

working at home

People these days no longer have a "job for life," but expect to undertake a series of careers or occupations throughout their working years. This means that they have to be much more prepared to change and grow, redevelop certain areas of their life, and constantly restructure the way in which they work.

SEE THE SIGNALS If you are self-employed and are not surrounded by colleagues who can give you signs that you have to retrain or restructure the way you work, you have to take the signals from clients and the regularity of payments coming in. If these are becoming erratic and you find yourself sitting around helplessly waiting for the phone to ring, you need to take your power back.

If your mailbox seems less full than usual, it may be time to restructure your working practices and recover your power.

MAKE CHANGES To regain control, rearrange your workspace so that you are in a more powerful position in your room. Instead of waiting for the work to come to you, reassess your standing, get yourself into a position of power, and signal that you are prepared to change.

REORGANIZE YOUR SPACE Consider where the room you work in is placed in relation to the front door and then try to line yourself up with good, direct, but not too fast flowing chi. If your office is at the top of your house in a back bedroom, move it to a more energized room, even if it involves radical reorganization. Then seat yourself in the most powerful part of the room. If you've been doing intricate work in a quiet area, looking at a wall, turn your desk around so that it's facing a door or a window to get more inspiration and energy. Write down five reasons why you love what you do and pin it up within sight of your desk to keep yourself motivated.

MOVE ON Consider letting go of things that are no longer supporting you, but do it with gratitude. So, as the final check for a project comes in, give a ceremonial thank you to the universe, acknowledging that you have come to the end of that particular task.

INVITE OPPORTUNITY Clear out some space on your desk or workspace for new files and opportunities. Introduce the color red into your work environment to give you courage and improve your self-esteem, because that will support you. Above all, trust that the universe will provide for you.

Good use of color and a few well-placed energizing objects in your office can help jump-start your career.

Facing a window attracts inspiration

Plants encourage the flow of chi

peace and quiet

In order to build a growing and successful career, it is important to have clarity of thought. To facilitate this, you need a place of quiet and stillness somewhere in the center of your home. Look after this area, and make sure that it is kept uncluttered, still, and calm.

The snake's capacity for stillness and contrasting fearless, fast movement have made it a powerful symbol in Chinese philosophy.

THE SNAKE In Chinese thinking, this central area of calm is often illustrated by the coiled snake, which represents deep wisdom and knowledge. The snake is very adaptable to its environment and can remain still and quiet when required, but at the same time, when it needs to act, it moves very quickly and without fear.

Ceaseless activity with no time for relaxation or quiet reflection breaks up energy flow, causing negative moods and behavior.

THE WHIRLWIND The opposite situation to this is created by allowing a whirlwind to develop in the center of your home. This kind of chaos is quite common, and frequently occurs in very yang households where the parents and the children are constantly away from home,

engaged in lots of different activities. A rush of activity can work fine in the short-term, but in the long-term, those involved will begin to lose their center and direction. Children will become burned out, angry, and difficult, and parents will feel unsupported and overburdened by their responsibilities.

QUIET SPACE Honoring this quiet area in your home will prevent a whirlwind from developing. It will also enable you to know when to keep your head down and plod along quietly at work, and when to make your move and change with the times. With the rapidity of change in modern working environments, this is important in helping you to maintain your status quo in the workplace.

Set an area aside— a spare room if you have one, or just a peaceful corner—to be used solely as a quiet space.

CASE STUDY

I was once called in to a consultation by a successful businesswoman who had moved into a new house and installed a very large rotor-bladed fan on the hallway ceiling as a decorative feature. The fan automatically started turning as soon as anyone entered the house, and it visually dominated the hall. However, she'd started to lose direction in her home and at work, and found that she couldn't think clearly anymore. We pinpointed the time that this had started to happen—just after she had installed the fan, which was constantly stirring up the chi in the household. Although she was very reluctant to do so, I persuaded her to switch the fan off—and six months later, she reappeared at one of my courses. She had been so impressed by the efficacy of the remedy that she'd decided to become a Feng Shui consultant!

QUICK FIXES

1. Clear the clutter out of your briefcase or work bag.

2. Go through your address book or Rolodex and delete any outdated addresses.

3. Keep your desk clear and put something beautiful on it to inspire you.

4. Take something to do with work into your home and see how it makes you feel.

5. If you work at home, site your office in an alcove or an extension.

happiness
and
well-being

Perhaps you believe Feng Shui won't work for you,
because you live in the "wrong" kind of house or
because your partner doesn't like you to move the
furniture around. Maybe you are always on the move
and think you don't have time for it. However, you can
use Feng Shui to increase your level of guilt-free
happiness in any environment .

daring to be happy

Everyone wants to feel happy—don't they? Well, no, not necessarily. We all have the potential to be happy, but many of us refuse to let ourselves enjoy life, often because of a firm belief— implanted in childhood—that we don't deserve to.

We all have a belief system that helps us to interpret the world around us, but some of those beliefs can hold us back.

QUESTIONS TO ASK YOURSELF

1. Do you believe you have the right to be happy?

2. Do you expect a negative payback from fate if you are happy?

3. How will it affect the significant people in your life if you become happy?

4. Are you prepared to risk being happy?

5. What will change in your life if you become more consistently happy?

IT'S YOUR RIGHT A lot of people don't believe, deep down, that they have the right to be happy, because they feel that state is something that has to be earned. Or perhaps they just don't think that they are good enough people to be happy. To enjoy happiness, it's important to separate it from the concept that it is the just deserts of the virtuous.

GUILT Guilt spoils the enjoyment of happiness. Happy feelings are often undermined by forebodings that something bad will happen to compensate for the current good times. Others feel that it is almost immoral to be happy when there is so much misery in the world.

True happiness does not depend on our achievements—it is about living life to the fullest and enjoying the here and now.

COURAGE Happiness requires courage. When you are happy, there is no excuse for not trying to achieve your ambitions. Unhappiness can be an excuse to put your life on hold or a way of holding a relationship together. Some people have an emotional investment in supporting unhappy friends or family in an unspoken collusion, which is destroyed when unhappiness is shaken off.

RELEASE If you are feeling unhappy, think hard about the questions on the previous page. If you can work out what it is that is holding you back, you can let it go.

learning to negotiate time and space

Feng Shui is about much more than simply arranging space; it is also about negotiating time and space together. Our ability to do this successfully means being in the right place at the right time; we have to be very conscious of the things that are going on around us and of our feelings in relationship to those events.

THE COMFORT ZONE Change is part of the nature of life, and our ability to grow and move on needs to be reflected in our living space. To improve your skill in negotiating time and space, look at the devices you surround yourself with to dampen down your feelings. We all create structures and routines to ward off unpleasant emotions, whether it is a compulsory cup of coffee in the morning or an essential martini in the evening. We derive comfort from old, familiar pieces of furniture such as squashy armchairs, so our houses become rigid in terms of routine and layout. People hooked on comfort cram their lives with activity so they don't have time to feel anything. Their houses are full of possessions: they often hoard reminders of past achievements, such as college books that they will never open again, or a collection of childish cuddly toys.

It can be difficult to give up the emotional buffer of comfortable, familiar furniture.

Wake up your senses by letting go of your comfort zone and experiencing real life.

NUMBNESS   Comfort is a good thing in moderate doses, but when it starts to dominate your life, it not only reduces your levels of pain but also numbs your capacity to feel. As a result the ability to experience joy, contentment, delight, and wonder—and therefore happiness, which is a mixture of all of these things— becomes severely diminished.

WAKE UP!   You can use Feng Shui to wake yourself up to happiness by realigning your perspective on life. The objective is to move away from the craving to create comfort and toward the desire to wake up to feeling. This means that you may also have to accept a number of difficult, challenging emotions—and be confident that you can handle them. To achieve this, you need to create a safe environment in which you can grow and change and handle difficult experiences, but your new surroundings will also have to be geared toward a broader experience of life, acting as a springboard to more joyous feelings.

trading in comfort for happiness

It's natural to want to make our living space as comfortable as possible, for ourselves and for our family and friends. But too much comfort can be a bad thing, because it may shrink our horizons and limit our opportunities for growth.

SAFETY Look around your living space and assess how much it is a comfort zone and how much a safe place. Try to move away from comfort and toward safety. Remove the throws and cushions from your armchairs, and make some empty space, to be filled with new opportunities for happiness.

Remove a few soft furnishings from your living room—they could be numbing your desire to experience life in the outside world.

UNLIMITED GROWTH Think of two seedlings, one planted in a pot, kept indoors, the other rooted in a flowerbed. The indoor plant is sheltered from bad weather; the other experiences gentle breezes and sunshine, as well as cold and rain. The development of the indoor plant is constrained by its pot, while outdoors, the possibilities for growth are unlimited.

DEPENDENCY Consider the tactics you use to fend off real feelings, like manipulation, repetitive behavior or dependencies used to mask pain. In an uncomfortable situation, one person may instantly turn on the TV; another might rush to phone a close friend and try to

persuade him or her to deal with the problem; someone else might simply reach for a bottle of wine. All you actually need to do is to recognize how you feel, take responsibility for it, and do something about it. Taking responsibility for things that make you uncomfortable enables you to take responsibility for being happy and work out how to move toward that state.

We use all sorts of distractions to avoid responsibility for really living our life. Find the courage to go without some of them.

GENUINE JOY Learn to distinguish between the things that genuinely bring you joy and inspiration and the things that just make you feel pain-free, cozy, and numb. If you become conscious of what makes you feel good or bad you can begin to consciously move toward feeling good more often. When you can do this successfully, you've learned how to live in space and time—and you will know where the right place at the right time is for you.

portable feng shui

You can start practicing being in the right space at the right time throughout your entire everyday existence. It is a valuable, broad principle, and is not only connected to arranging your space at home—you can learn to read your whole life in a different way.

STICK TO YOUR DECISIONS Be determined to do one thing in spite of every single sign that you shouldn't do it (within reason, of course!). For example, decide to go on a picnic and stick to your decision, in spite of friends suggesting alternative activities, or not being able to find the picnic basket, or the weather looking less than promising. Learn when to go with the flow and when to stand firm.

TAKE RESPONSIBILITY You should also be aware of how to position yourself. When you move into a new environment, look carefully at

Your attitude to an event matters more than the event itself.

your surroundings with Feng Shui eyes and decide where the function you are about to perform in it will be best served. You should be constantly conscious of how you feel about what you're doing, and instead of getting yourself into an uncomfortable position and then lapsing into one of your customary devices for deadening your feelings, take responsibility for not allowing yourself to get into that position in the first place. And if you do accidentally drop into it, take a moment to clarify your thoughts, then admit to yourself: "This isn't working for me" and move out of the situation.

STAND FIRM When you walk into a restaurant, for example, decide on what kind of time you want to spend there; whether you want to be stimulated or relaxed. Then look around and decide which area offers the best space for the result you are after. Consider what will be supporting your back (if anything) and what you will be facing. If you want to be stimulated, you should sit toward the front of the restaurant where the brighter lights are, in the window space, or in a very central position. If you want a quieter time, sit in a recess or secluded corner and avoid being on the route to the washroom, kitchen, bar, or main door, where you will be disturbed by lots of activity. And if the right space for you is already occupied by someone else, have the courage to say, "I need to eat somewhere else," because eating there won't be the best use of your time.

A crowded avenue of restaurants is the right space if you're looking for stimulation.

A quiet table for two is the right space if you want to relax.

feng shui away from home

Your vacation destination can become a home away from home if you apply a few simple Feng Shui principles.

Perhaps you spend a lot of time away from home traveling for business or pleasure. No problem! You can still continue to practice Feng Shui, even when you are in a strange environment. Learn how to continue to nurture yourself, even when you are staying somewhere unfamiliar a long way from home.

INSIDE THE HOTEL When you check into a hotel, be aware of what kind of room you are agreeing to accept. There are a number of features to avoid.

You may not sleep well if the bed has a mirror facing it, because the activity of the chi bouncing between your body and the glass will prevent you from relaxing properly.

Mirror facing bed

Heavy furniture around bed

Challenging Feng Shui is common in basic hotel rooms.

If the end of the bed is pointing at the door, you may wake up feeling drained of energy, because the chi will flow from you out into the corridor, leaving you feeling very depleted or even ill.

Heavy furniture looming over the bed has the effect of a person craning over you all night, so you may end up feeling constricted and cramped and are likely to wake up suffering from a fuzzy head or a headache.

An adjoining bathroom carved out of the corner of the room rather than running alongside it is very depleting, because chi is being discharged in a room where you are supposed to be resting. You would be better off having to use a communal bathroom down the corridor.

Once you start to realize the impact that different spatial arrangements have on your life, it will give you the courage to say, "No, I don't want this room, I'd like to see another one," and you might choose to spend more money to secure a

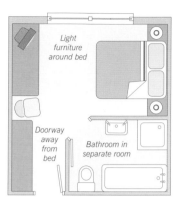

Light furniture around bed

Doorway away from bed

Bathroom in separate room

bigger, more suitable room with a well-placed bathroom to ensure a good night's sleep, while economizing elsewhere.

Good Feng Shui will lead to a restful night's sleep.

OUTSIDE THE HOTEL Remember to look out of the window of the room to check whether it is in line with any angles of cutting chi or large, threatening structures, because these will also contribute to a bad night's sleep.

An unobstructed view from a hotel window will be conducive to a restful stay.

185

feng shui on the move

Feng Shui is not necessarily confined to static buildings; it can still be practiced when you are traveling. It may sound laughable, but you can even use Feng Shui in a subway car! So look around before you take your seat, and settle in the best position in which to be nurtured while you are traveling to your destination.

ON THE SUBWAY Rather than slumping into the first available seat on the subway, take a good look around. You will find that there is a supported area with the Tortoise to the back, and this may be anything from closed doors to a bench seat. Part of the car will offer a better view of the window, representing the Phoenix.

Take responsibility for the positions you find yourself in: only you can change them.

Again, avoid the seats closest to the washroom or a place near a door, where people will constantly be passing in front of you. The old idea of sitting facing the direction you are traveling in is a sound one, because it means that all the support and driving force is behind you, moving you forward.

TRAVELING COMPANIONS Sit next to someone who appears non-threatening. If you realize that you are constantly setting up situations where you end up fighting for your space or dealing with intimidation, ask yourself whether this is a pattern that is apparent in your whole life. Some people consistently set up difficult situations like this, just to

prove to themselves that they can handle it—perhaps because they have had to cope with a lot of difficulty or look after themselves unassisted in the past. You can change the message that you give yourself about your life by choosing to place yourself in good positions. There is nothing to prove; you deserve to feel safe and secure.

Feng Shui principles will help you identify a comfortable space to rest from the excessive yang of a busy street.

ON THE STREET Even if you stop while walking down the street, be aware of where and why you've come to a standstill. If you feel like a rest, make sure that you have your back against some support, so that you feel nurtured.

SPACE AND ENERGY Wherever you go and whatever you do, try, at all times, to be aware of space and energy and what effect they are having on you, because if you are not being supported, you are being depleted. If you constantly endeavor to move into a better space, you are nurturing yourself and building yourself up, and you'll find that your need to seek out comfort will be reduced as the feeling of being awake and alive becomes more familiar.

learning to receive
the gift of difficulty

Life is not about achieving perfection, it is about embracing everything that comes our way as an opportunity to grow and move on. So learn to accept any challenges and difficulties as a gift that will help you in your future development.

EXCUSES, EXCUSES Lots of times when I am teaching or consulting, people tell me that Feng Shui won't work for them for a number of reasons. Perhaps they reside in a very "difficult" living space or a badly situated house. Maybe they didn't choose their living space, because they moved in with a partner or they inherited or are renting the property. Alternatively, they may share their space with someone who is completely unprepared to clutter-clear or move their possessions around. In fact, these are not valid reasons for not practicing Feng Shui.

Other people's clutter can be a convenient excuse for not taking control of your home environment.

"BAD" FENG SHUI People often concentrate on their home's weaknesses and ignore its strengths. Feng Shui is often fear-based, and people worry about their houses. A typical phone call to me will go, "I know something is wrong, but I don't know what to do about it," rather than "I live in a fantastic space, but I've got a bit of an issue with one of the rooms." There is no such thing as bad Feng Shui—every house will teach us something.

Occupants of spacious houses can be as unhappy about "bad" Feng Shui as those who live in cramped surroundings. With a little effort, both types of space can work equally well.

SPACE THAT WORKS We can read our outer space as an expression of who we are, reflecting our own strengths or weaknesses, and we can take responsibility for being there. Every home is going to have plus points, even if it is only that the rent is low. It may be small, but small can be made to feel either cramped or cozy.

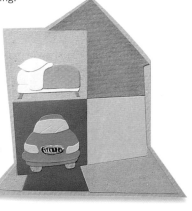

seeing problems as gifts

I was always taught that every problem is a gift and the bigger the problem, the bigger the gift. This is something that has carried me through for years, because it's absolutely true. Apply the philosophy to your life and you will also learn how valuable it is.

Look after your health by reassessing your situation whenever you feel stuck. Make changes that will re-create well-being.

SEE THE CHALLENGE Look at your home's supposed weaknesses as challenges. If you have small, easily solvable problems in your space, it's good, because you can improve your situation easily. If they're big problems, the potential for change in your life is huge.

SEE THE BIGGER PICTURE If there is a big brick wall outside your front door, don't see it as a feature that only belongs to the house, but ask yourself how the feature relates to your life. Does it mean that there is an equally solid brick wall blocking your future? And if so, why have you put it there? What purpose does it serve for you? Is it actually quite useful because it's forcing you to keep reassessing your current situation? Is it making you physically unwell, so that you have to reinterpret your life to ensure your health improves in the long-term?

CHANGE PERSPECTIVE Even those classic Feng Shui problems, such as having a bathroom situated in the southeast corner of your home, can be seen as a useful challenge. If this is the case in your house, it means that a lot of energy is moving out of that area very fast. Consequently, you may need to pay attention to one particular area of your life and let go of something. That could be your hostility toward someone who's done you wrong in the past, or your desire to become a world-class athlete, which has become unrealistic now that you have reached middle age. If it's the latter, interpret this sign as an opportunity to do something new and different, while employing everything you learned while training to be an athlete.

Face up to your unachievable dreams, and take swift action to move on.

LISTEN TO YOUR INNER VOICE

Maybe what you've got to let go of is your inability to move forward from your past, which is preventing you from being creative and happy in the present. If you can hear a voice saying to you, "You don't need to be successful" or "I love you the way you are," whose voice is it that you are hearing? Try to work out what it is that's keeping you from moving on—and then let it go.

Remove the clutter that connects you to your past. The energy these objects contain will hold you back.

toeing the feng shui line

It's easy to implement Feng Shui in the home when you live alone and don't have anyone else to consider. If you share your living space with other people, however, problems can easily arise— especially when the other occupants of your living space resist your suggestions because they are hostile to the notion of change.

FREE THE CONSTRAINTS Suppose you live with someone—whether it is a husband, wife, son, daughter, mother, or roommate—who refuses to cooperate with your attempts at Feng Shui. You may feel they are blocking your progress, but this is actually a wonderful gift, because it gives you the chance to look at why you're in that relationship. You can use the disagreement as a talking point to untangle the ways in which that other person constrains you throughout the rest of your life.

Holding on to useless objects is a way of avoiding the pain involved in changing your circumstances.

BE SUPPORTIVE If this person won't get rid of any clutter, ask him or her to choose the least offensive object—anything from a paper bag to a dead plant—and ask how it would make him or her feel if you threw it away. Most people are not vindictive; what they are usually trying to do is avoid pain. If what you are suggesting is something that this person knows is going to be painful, the only way forward is to support him or her in coping.

ANTICIPATE OBJECTIONS Ask other occupants how they'd feel if you moved the sofa. They might say it's not going to work because it's not practical. If you gently persevere in asking them how it would feel to them if it was moved, they might reply that the room is going to be really bare without the sofa in its customary place. Then ask them how they would feel if the room was bare. Is it reminding them of a bare room in their past? If so, how did it make them feel then?

A sofa is a powerful symbol of comfort— moving it from its familiar position can become a very contentious issue!

OFFER UNDERSTANDING If it's your partner who's being obstructive, use it as an opportunity to help the relationship to grow. Sometimes you can end up really enjoying yourself in dismantling things, and it can be the beginning of a whole new period in the relationship. This can bring increased mutual understanding, and it's a huge relief to people to move through something that has been constricting them. You may also discover that you have been using your partner's attitude as an excuse for not making changes to enhance your own happiness.

honoring the home

Happiness is a practical reality. It's not just an experience we have in our head—it is a whole body experience, because we are not just spirits floating in ether. We have physical bodies, which need looking after, and our health and well-being are inextricably connected to how efficiently we nurture ourselves.

Honor your body and respect your mind by avoiding inappropriate relationships that drain your energy.

BODY AND MIND Our physical bodies are the route to our emotional and spiritual well-being, because the way we make contact with things on a physical level feeds information about how we feel about ourselves back to our emotions and our souls. It's very difficult to be in a state of perfect bliss and happiness when we are living in an abused body—a body we have little respect for. We often restrict and restrain our body and emotions, dulling them into numbness for the sake of comfort, or enmeshing them in a series of relationships we've set up to justify our perceived underachievement in an achievement-oriented society.

HONOR AND RESPECT Some people find it hard to honor and respect their bodies. They've been brought up to be severely critical of themselves, because they've been taught that achievement is all and just "being" is not sufficient. One way to begin the process of moving toward happiness is to practice honoring and respecting your outer environment and at every level, all the time. In other words, treat your living space in the way that you expect to be treated yourself.

A HEALTHY HOME Keep your home as clean as you can in a way that's as loving as possible. Don't blast it with chemicals that will kill off its energy and vitality. Try to use the best and most natural products to make your house feel fresh and lively. Choose the objects you want to keep in your house very carefully, and do not compromise. Have one beautiful thing rather than six substandard items. Remove any broken objects; after all, you wouldn't walk around with your body in a state of disrepair! You should apply the same care to maintaining your home as you do to maintaining your body.

The cleanliness of a house reflects the condition of the occupant's soul.

Maintain your surroundings and they will reward you with relaxation and calm.

changing with the seasons

When you are practicing Feng Shui, remember that you will never manage to arrange your surroundings into one perfect setting that will last for the rest of your life. Your life is in a constant state of change, and your home environment should reflect that.

The nature of your surroundings has far-reaching effects on your mind and body.

WORK ON THE OUTSIDE The wonderful thing about Feng Shui is that while it's difficult to change ourselves from the inside—to alter our diet, or increase our self-respect, or start looking for healthier relationships—it's often easier to start working on the outer environment by practicing Feng Shui on the home. You can begin by setting up affirmations and positive images in your home, and learning to treat your house in the way you'd like to be treated yourself. The changes brought about in your immediate surroundings will help to bring about changes in many other areas of your life.

SEASONAL CYCLES Start to see your home as a changing and constantly evolving space rather than as something static. A good way to begin is to get in touch with the natural cycle by changing your house with the seasons. Bring back the old-fashioned idea of having summer and winter curtains;

Reflect the seasonal changes of earth's natural cycle by ringing the changes inside your home.

in the summer, hang muslin at your windows; in the winter, use heavy, rich velvet. Place thicker rugs on the floor in the winter, and when summer comes take them up, clean them, and put them into storage. Change your bedding between the seasons too. Rearrange the seating areas around the windows and doors in summer, and around sources of heat and light in the winter, then play around with subtle modulations during the transition times of spring and autumn. Allow your house to move with the seasons.

CASE STUDY

Your home should reflect how you yourself are growing and changing, so avoid fixing lots of rigid, built-in furniture to the walls. I remember going to a consultation in a very affluent apartment building. The owner of the apartment I looked at was desperate to change but was completely stuck in her life and could see no way of moving forward. Although the cause of the problem was obvious, it was a very difficult consultation—because almost all of the furniture in her home was built in. There was virtually nothing I could advise her to do—apart from ripping it all out! As she spent most of her waking hours in the apartment, it's no wonder she felt stultified.

setting up
positive images

Everything we do, say, and think will exist in the universe at some
point and become real, so you can influence the kind of energy that
flows around you. If you create a positive environment, you will
increase the levels of positive energy
around you, so try to ensure you have
beautiful objects of a high quality in your
home that will inspire you.

CHOOSE THE RIGHT ARTWORK On a very
basic level, don't hang any negative images on the walls
of your home, because pictures symbolize your
aspirations. A classic but subtle example of this is the
single person who hangs up lots of pictures of deserted
winter landscapes or of one person sitting alone at a café
table or of one person walking away from another person.
These images creep into the subconscious and attract
similar energy. If you are looking for a relationship, you
should hang up pictures that convey feelings of fun,
happiness, and good times, featuring couples together,
nurturing and loving situations, and sunny,
happy days.

*Choose pictures that
illustrate your hopes
for the future.*

PRACTICE APPRECIATION Keep your living space
alive. If you don't know what else to do, create a bare
room, take all the furniture out of it, and then spend 24

hours—or 20 minutes, whatever you can bear!—in it, thinking about what makes you happy about that room. Then move back in only those things usually in the room

Decorate your house with objects that make you happy.

that make you happy. You may really appreciate your wardrobe once it's been taken out of the bedroom—or you may decide that you don't miss it at all and would rather leave it on the landing outside.

TAKE IT EASY If you don't have the time, strength, or inclination to get involved in shifting a room full of furniture, you can identify which objects make you happy by standing at the door of the room and mentally clearing it out!

CASE STUDY

I once did a consultation with a woman who had lots of reproductions of Pre-Raphaelite paintings around her house. They featured beautiful women, but many of the subjects were inspired by tragic stories. She had collected them over the years and was very attached to them, so I suggested she first let go of the one she liked least and consider replacing it with something happier, then continue the process until the sad pictures were balanced by cheerful ones. Pictures of death are acceptable if they are balanced by positive images, because death is part of life—but it's not the only thing in life.

life as a journey

Hopefully, by now you will have learned the ways in which we can use Feng Shui as a tool to achieve balance and harmony within our lives. It is not a cureall, but it can help us to tackle persistent problems that are holding us back from fulfilling our full potential.

Step into the common flow of energy that we all share, and open your life up to new people and fresh experiences.

EMBRACE YOUR CHALLENGES Life is a continuing process and provides plenty of scope to grow and change all the time, so as problems come our way, we should embrace them. They can be used as a springboard for further development and achieving a truly joyful position. When you feel safe enough to open up to love and give it to other people, then you become part of a community in which there is an easy flow between individuals and between different parts of your own self.

GO WITH THE FLOW Chi needs to be able to move easily, not only in our outer space, but also in our inner space. If we create a living space in which we can give and receive acceptance, a space that is available to our friends, a space that allows movement, flow, and growth, we can become a part of this process rather than standing resentfully to one side watching others participate in life without trying to join in.

CASE STUDY

I did a consultation with a wealthy woman who lived in a beautiful house where all the blinds and curtains were drawn during the day. She said it was because of the road noise at the front, and because the sun would fade the furnishings at the back. She had also decorated throughout with beige. She rarely left the house and spent most of her time ironing. I suggested opening the curtains and introducing color into her home. She did as I suggested, and the next time I visited, she was a changed person, with a new outlook on life.

GROW AND DEVELOP It is within our power to create living spaces that will make this ideal situation a real possibility, and that will support us in what we are trying to do and also support those around us. We should be able to feel confident of using any space that we arrive in, knowing that it will support us. We should be able to recognize that while there are desirable and necessary boundaries around our personal space, we can let other people into it if we wish—and they will leave again when we choose.

This is really the explanation for why so many people are practicing Feng Shui every moment of their lives. They see it as a means of self-development and growth—and they have discovered for themselves that it works.

Feng Shui is a powerful way to make your life flower with abundant new growth.

QUICK FIXES

1. List seven positive attributes about your house, and then decide on the top three.

2. Clear out a room of your house and only put back the things that truly make you happy.

3. If time is short, tidy a drawer or cupboard instead.

4. Ask an honest friend to help you clutter-clear all your clothes, from shoes to jewelry, to increase your vitality.

5. Arrange a spring cleaning by a specialist company and bring someone else's energy into your home.

glossary

CHI The invisible breath of energy, or life force, that pervades everything in the universe.

DRAGON This celestial animal represents the energy of the east and the element wood.

EARTH Earth energy represents relationships, nurturing, the ability to be centered, and resourcefulness; it is associated with natural earth colors and with the central direction.

ELEMENTS In Chinese belief five elements (earth, wood, metal, water, and fire) are associated with Feng Shui; they symbolize certain actions, conditions of the mind, and seasons.

FIRE Fire energy represents action, enlightenment, self-esteem, and public status; it is associated with flame colors and with the direction south.

METAL Metal energy represents order, leisure and pleasure, structure, and creativity; it is associated with white, silver, and gold, and with the direction west.

PHOENIX This celestial animal represents the energy of the south and the element fire.

TIGER This celestial animal represents the energy of the west and the element metal.

TORTOISE This celestial animal represents the energy of the north and the element water.

WATER Water energy represents contemplation and quiet; it is associated with blue and black, and with the direction north.

WOOD Wood energy represents growth, development, and planning; it is associated with the color green, and with the direction east.

YANG Creative energy, perceived as active, masculine, hot, and sharp; its complementary opposite is Yin and, together with Yin, it is present in all things in life.

YIN Receptive energy, perceived as passive, feminine, soft, and cold; its complementary opposite is Yang and, together with Yang, it is present in all things in life.

further reading

CF Baynes, Richard Wilhelm (trans.)
The I Ching or Book of Changes
Princeton University Press, 1992

Master Lam Kam Chuen
The Feng Shui Handbook Henry Holt,
1996

Alison Daniels
Feng Shui for You and Your Cat
Watson–Guptill, 1999

Stephen L. Karcher
How to Use the I Ching
Element Books, 1998

Karen Kingston
Clear Your Clutter with Feng Shui
Broadway Books, 1999

Karen Kingston
*Creating Sacred Space with Feng
Shui* Broadway Books, 1996

Mishio Kushi
Nine Star Ki One Peaceful World,
1992

Gina Lazenby
The Feng Shui House Book
Watson–Guptill, 1998

Denise Linn
*Sacred Space: Clearing and
Enhancing the Energy of Your Home*
Ballentine Books, 1996

Jan Sandifer
Feng Shui Astrology Piatkus, 1999

Stephen Skinner
The Living Earth Manual of Feng Shui
Arkana, 1990

William Spear
Feng Shui Made Easy
Harper, 1995

Gerry Thompson
Feng Shui Astrology for Lovers
Sterling, 1998

Lao Tsu
Tao Te Ching Vintage Books,
1997

R. L. Wing
The Illustrated I Ching
Doubleday, 1982

Takashi Yoshikawa
The Ki Trafalgar Square, 1998

useful addresses

AUSTRALASIA

FENG SHUI DESIGN STUDIO
PO Box 7788 Bondi Beach
Sydney 2026 Australia
Tel: 61 2 9365 7877
Fax: 61 2 9365 7847

FENG SHUI CONSULTANTS
PO Box 34160
Birkenhead
Auckland
New Zealand
Tel: 64 9 483 7513

GREAT BRITAIN

FENG SHUI ASSOCIATION
31 Woburn Place
Brighton BN1 9GA
Tel/fax: 44 1273 693844

FENG SHUI COMPANY
Ballard House
37 Norway Street
Greenwich
London SE10 9DD

FENG SHUI FOUNDATION
(Jane Butler-Biggs)
PO Box 1640
Hassocks
East Sussex BN6 9ZT
E-mail:
fengshui.foundation@virgin.net

FENG SHUI SOCIETY
377 Edgware Road
London W2 1BT
Tel: 07050–289 2000
Web site: www.fengshuisociety.org.uk

CANADA

CANADIAN FENG SHUI CENTRE
1465 Dewbourne Crescent
Burlington
Ontario L7M IE8
Web site: www.fengshui.ca

NORTH AMERICA

EARTH DESIGN
PO Box 530725
Miami Shores
FL 33153
Tel: 1 305 756 6426
Fax: 1 305 751 9995

FENG SHUI DESIGNS INC.
PO Box 399
Nevada City
CA 95959
Tel/fax: 1 800 551 2482

THE FENG SHUI INSTITUTE OF AMERICA
PO Box 488
Wabasso
FL 32970
Tel: 1 561 589 9900
Fax: 1 561 589 1611

FENG SHUI WAREHOUSE
PO Box 6689
San Diego
CA 92166
Tel: 1 619 523 2158
Fax: 1 619 523 2165

index

index

acknowledgments

The publishers are grateful to the following for permission to reproduce copyright material.

Abode UK: pp. 103, 109T, 123T, 127T, 133T, 189, 195, 199

Corbis: pp. 14B, 15T, 22B, 23, 27T, 39T, 40B, 43, 74, 75T, 97T, 129, 131, 134, 136, 181T, 191B, 196

Liz Eddison: pp. 107, 139B

Image Bank: pp. 11B, 19B, 44, 52B, 61B, 77B, 98, 101, 172B

Images Color Library: pp. 69T, 83

Stock Market: pp. 26, 29T, 91, 154, 162, 183

Tony Stone: pp. 2, 12, 56B, 62, 67B, 70, 80, 85T, 90, 118, 121T, 122B, 142, 147, 151B, 157, 165, 166B, 173, 176, 177, 179, 185, 187, 188, 194, 200

Thanks are due to the following for help in supplying properties and materials.

Collingwood and Bachellor, Horley

Bright Ideas, Lewes

Louis Potts and Company, Lewes

Spoils, Crawley

Baltic Trader, Lewes